21st May —

ADELAID]

C000108874

ayah = maid,
care of children

coolie = local man
hired for cheap
labour

DAY BY DAY AT LUCKNOW

A JOURNAL

OF THE

SIEGE OF LUCKNOW

Elibron Classics
www.elibron.com

DAY BY DAY AT LUCKNOW.

A JOURNAL

OF THE

SIEGE OF LUCKNOW.

BY MRS. CASE

WIDOW OF COLONEL CASE, 32ND REGT. (QUEEN'S).

William

LONDON

RICHARD BENTLEY, NEW BURLINGTON STREET

Publisher in Ordinary to Her Majesty

1858

LONDON
PRINTED BY SPOTTISWOODE AND CO.
NEW-STREET SQUARE

PREFACE.

In submitting the following pages for public inspection, I have listened to the suggestions of my friends rather than to the dictates of my own judgment. They were written for the perusal of my relatives in England, and with no view whatever to publication; and it was not without a struggle in my own mind that I at last complied with their wishes. They represented to me, that but few journals had survived the siege of Lucknow and the wreck of the steamer which conveyed us from India, and that any particulars of that protracted and dreadful beleaguerment would be read with great interest by the friends and relatives of those who fought and bled in that ill-fated city.

I have not attempted, by subsequent additions, to produce effect, or to aim at glowing descriptions, but have given it as it was written, in the simple narrative form, which the dangers and privations of the siege alone permitted. As I do not aspire to the ambition of an author, I feel that I shall be exempted from that criticism which invariably attends works of a more pretending character. It cannot but fail (for no woman is equal to the task) to do justice to the heroism, or to describe in adequate terms the great sufferings, of the gallant defenders of Lucknow, but it will help to fill up, by particulars, the general outline of the contest, which has been heretofore published in official despatches, and partially gratify the curiosity of those who have sympathised with us in our severe trials, until some more able and more practised person shall undertake the task of favouring the world with a complete and detailed history.

ADELAIDE CASE.

June 5th, 1858.

ERRATA.

NARRATIVE

&c.

CHAPTER I.

Thursday, May 21st, 1857.

For several weeks past much anxiety had been felt by us all at Lucknow, in consequence of the alarming rumours respecting the mutinous state of the Indian Army. The ladies scarcely knew that things looked so dark and gloomy as they really did; but I must confess my fear on the subject was more roused by the serious way in which I used to hear dear William, who was always bright and cheerful under any circumstances, talk over affairs with Colonel Inglis, than from what I read in the papers.

On Saturday, the 16th of May, there was a consultation amongst the senior officers as to what had better be done, as they were in doubt whether the sepoys in the station would be true ; and if they mutinied, it was thought the city would also rise.   The result was, that, in the course of the day, the 32nd Regiment received an order to occupy the Residency in the city, a commanding position, containing the treasury and all the public offices ; and in the evening they sent in, as a support to the sepoy guard, 130 men and four guns, with all their sick, and women, and children.   The following day, Sunday the 17th, the remainder of the regiment marched to cantonments, and encamped under some trees ; the thermometer 110°, and a dust storm.

There had been a rumour in the night that

the sepoys were about to burn and kill, and
we afterwards heard that all the ladies had
rushed to the Residency, but it was a false
alarm.   Sir Henry Lawrence had most
kindly offered to put up the ladies of the
32nd Regiment (we were only four) at the
Residency in cantonments; consequently we
were busy packing up our things the whole
of Saturday, and I was dreadfully knocked
up, Caroline helping me with her usual kindness and activity.   William, of course, was
obliged to be attending more to his regi-
mental duties than to us.   We were told that
we must be ready to mount our horses at
three o'clock on Sunday morning, as we were
to go with the regiment into cantonments.

I think it must have been twelve o'clock
before I went to bed, as we had packed up
every thing but our furniture.   I had not
slept an hour, when I was roused up by
Colonel Inglis's voice calling William, who

instantly jumped up to see what was the matter. I felt very nervous and frightened, and when he came back I heard that a rumour was afloat that the regiment was to be attacked on its way into cantonments. William, of course, hastily dressed and went off to the regiment, leaving injunctions that Caroline and I were not to start till he returned. I went instantly to Caroline's room and found her getting up, as she had been restless owing to the great heat, and, like myself, rather nervous; for indeed it would be difficult for any one to realise our sensations who had not experienced them on that dreadful morning.

We were soon equipped and ready to mount our steeds; our good and faithful servants doing their best to make us as comfortable as they could. The ayah had our tea and bread and butter as nicely brought in as if we had been going out for our usual

morning's ride. When we had been ready
some little time we began to get impatient
that William did not return for us. At last
I could bear the waiting no longer, so
mounting my horse, and taking my syce with
me, I went over to Mrs. Inglis in the next
compound, but finding her not ready to start,
I returned. The scene at this time was
truly curious. The moon was shining
brightly, and all the servants were busily
engaged loading the hackeries which were to
take our things to the station. Several
chokedars had been sent down to take care
of the house, gardens, and property which
we left behind us. They were all armed.
Every thing was carried on as quietly as possible, so as not to excite the suspicion of the
city people. As all these preparations were
going on, the sensations I felt as I sat quietly
on my horse are perfectly indescribable.
Caroline's horse was lame, so she could not

ride him; but Colonel Inglis most kindly
lent her one of his horses, " Waverley,"
and as soon as he was brought over she
mounted, and we both went over to Mrs.
Inglis. Still William had not returned, and
the moments passed anxiously away. At
last Mrs. Inglis proposed our riding up the
road in the direction of the city. The children were placed in her carriage, and my ayah
went in ours; Mrs. Giddings, the paymaster's
wife, went in a buggy. I confess that I was
very much frightened, but my courage all
returned when, after waiting for nearly an
hour from the time when we were first
ready, we saw dear William coming towards
us, and then we all galloped up as fast
as we could to the spot where our escort
was. This consisted of an advanced guard
of cavalry and the 32nd Regiment. The
ladies were in the centre, and the 32nd in the
rear. We reached the Residency in canton-

ments safely about 6 A.M., all tired and exhausted.

The time appeared long till breakfast, but as soon as William had seen all right in camp, for with him his soldiers were ever his first object, he came to the Residency, about ten o'clock, to see how Carry and I were getting on. Much to his horror, he found us in a dark room, without a window in it, the only light we had coming in from the bath-room. We were, however, soon afterwards removed to a very comfortable one, through the kindness of Sir Henry Lawrence, who, though so much occupied with weighty and important matters, thought nothing too trifling for him to attend to. He insisted on our going with him to the different rooms in his house, and gave us the choice of any we liked, provided we made ourselves comfortable, which he wished us to do before any one else arrived; so Carry and I were soon settled in a very nice cool room, with a punkah and tatties. The officers of the sepoy regiments turned out of their messes and houses to give them up to the 32nd men, and the camp is moved much nearer the European artillery. William came to breakfast and dinner, so I am as happy as I can be under the circumstances. With Mrs. Inglis and her three dear boys, we are a cheerful little party. In the evening, whenever we can, we go into the camp and spend, at any rate, one happy hour with our husbands, sitting in the cool semianah, where they generally have iced water and sherry for us, and dear Johnny amuses himself with looking at the different tents and the horses, &c., with the bearer.

Tuesday, 26th.

WE have been subjected to constant alarms during the last few days. Sometimes it was a panic amongst the ladies in the station, who got frightened with the continual reports that the city was going to rise, when they rushed over to the Residency for safety ; then it was an alarm of fire. One evening these wretches did set fire to a building behind the Residency just as we were sitting down to dinner, but most providentially the wind changed, and their intention, which had evidently been to burn the Residency, was thus frustrated. So constant, however, was the terror in which we were kept on this subject, that we always had a little bundle ready by our bedsides at night, for instant flight.

Yesterday morning, Monday, I was awoke
about three o'clock by Mrs. Inglis coming
into our room, and telling us that we must
immediately get up ; as, in consequence of
Sir Henry Lawrence having received un-
favourable accounts of the state of things at
Cawnpore, it was deemed by him to be safer
for us ladies to go into the city Residency.
We were all to start as soon as possible, so I
roused up Caroline, and we dressed as hastily
as we could, leaving our few things to be
packed up by my good ayah, who, with the
rest of the servants, was to follow in the
course of the day. As soon as we were
dressed, William came over from the camp,
and, as usual, on seeing him and hearing the
cheerful sound of his voice, I was inspired
with renewed courage. He could only remain with us a few minutes, as he did not
like to be away from camp. Mrs. Inglis
and the children started about half an hour

before we did. We drove into the city in our little carriage; everything appeared quiet. We reached the city Residency in safety between six and seven o'clock, and found Mrs. Inglis already located at Mr. Gubbins's. We drove to his house first, and found Mrs. Gubbins, who kindly offered to do any thing for us that she could, but told us that her house was already full, and that Mrs. Inglis's room was too small to take us both in. She would most kindly have done so, had it been possible. We therefore went over to the Residency, accompanied by Mr. Edmonstone of the 32nd, where we saw Mrs. Ogilvie, whom we had known slightly, having met her at dinner at Sir Henry's. She said that there were no rooms to spare in the Residency upstairs, and on going below, we found it still more crowded. Two ladies and seven children were squeezed into a very small room, having some tea, and every moment fresh arrivals drove up, in search of rooms also. While we were deliberating what we had better do, Mrs. Ogilvie sent word to us to come up again, and then offered us one of her own rooms, which was so filled with boxes, books, and papers, that it seemed almost impossible to turn round in it. At the same time she told us, that we must not mind the bearer passing through the room at all hours of the day for the iced water used in the house, and for all his candles and lamps ; but of course we did not refuse her kind offer, considering ourselves fortunate in obtaining the smallest corner. We immediately set to work to clean out the space allowed us, and the things soon coming up with the ayah, we succeeded in making ourselves as comfortable as the circumstances would admit of. Nothing could exceed the kindness of Dr. and Mrs. Ogilvie.

Friday, 29th.

EVERY thing still remains quiet. Caroline
and I join the Ogilvies' party at dinner.
We see Mrs. Inglis every day, and she and I
think of nothing but our happy evening's
drive into cantonments, where we spend the
only delightful hour during the twenty-four.
She drives her buggy, and takes me with her.
People say we are very foolish to persist in
going to the camp in the present state of
things; but so long as our husbands do not
forbid our going out, we shall continue to do
so, for I think we would both risk almost any
danger for the sake of that one happy hour,
which always appears so very short! Oh,
how loth we always feel to return to the

Residency again !   How we linger before we
turn our steps towards the city, till Colonel
Inglis or William insists, for the sake of safety,
that we will not delay.

Monday, June 1st.

ON Saturday last, the 30th, Mrs. Inglis,
as usual, came, and asked me if I was ready
to drive into camp. Of course, I was. So
off we started about half-past five o'clock.
The day having been hot, we enjoyed our
drive exceedingly, and, as usual, found
William and Colonel Inglis sitting on the
semianah ready for us. We remained with
them a short time, and on coming away
Colonel Inglis said he would drive Mrs.
Inglis part of the way home, and William
drove me ; but they could not go far with us,
of course. When they left us, and we found

it begin to get rather late, and towards dusk, we felt uncomfortable, especially as we passed the Iron Bridge, a place always very much crowded. We fancied the people we saw looked fierce and sullen. Mrs. Inglis drove a fast trotting horse, neither of us spoke, but she urged him on. I cannot express how thankful we felt when we drew up at the door of the Residency, and alighted in safety. It is really surprising that we did so, for the mutiny in cantonments broke out that very evening, showing how rebellious the prevailing spirit must then have been.

Just as we were all retiring for the night, guns were heard in the direction of the cantonments. All the gentlemen immediately armed themselves and disappeared, leaving us very anxious. On going out into the verandah, we distinctly saw the firing, and saw one bungalow after another set on fire, and blazing away with tremendous fury. The

stillness in the city was very remarkable ; not
a sound was heard.   The sight of the burning bungalows was awful, and we could do
nothing but watch the flames with beating
hearts, and listen tremblingly to the booming
of the cannon.

About half-past eleven o'clock, the firing
diminished, and a sowar galloped up to the
Residency with a message from Sir Henry
Lawrence, to say that all was nearly over.   A
few minutes later, Mrs. Inglis sent me over
a line in pencil, which she had just received
from Colonel Inglis, telling her of his own
safety, and that of dearest William. Those only
who experienced the anxiety and terror of
that dreadful night can ever know the heartfelt gratitude we felt towards our Heavenly
Father for preserving our beloved ones
through so much danger.   We then retired
to our room, I cannot say to sleep, but anxiously to wait for the dawn of day.   Mrs.

Boileau and her eldest boy shared our room with us. They had come over with several other ladies from the Fayrers and Ommanneys' houses. Poor little Charlie laid down on my bed, but the child was so restless from the heat and anxiety, that he could not sleep.

The usual messenger from camp brought me, what I never failed to get every morning—a letter from dearest William. He told me that the sepoys had mutinied on the previous evening, and attempted to get hold of their officers, but failed. They then set fire to the bungalows and plundered them. Lieutenant Grant, of the 71st Native Infantry, was betrayed and cruelly murdered, receiving many wounds. Cornet Raleigh, a young officer who had only joined his regiment three days before, was cut to pieces by the cavalry, and Brigadier Hanscombe was shot dead as he went up to harangue the native regiment. A careless shot from one of our own guns went through William's tent, and killed Caroline's beautiful horse " Lalla," and wounded the poor " Sahib " so badly, that he was obliged to be shot next morning. Three of our poor servants were killed, and William's and Colonel Inglis's tents were riddled to shreds. I cannot say how much I feel for poor Caroline having lost her favourite horse. Mine was only saved by the syce having the good sense to take him away to a neighbouring village, where he kept him for a whole day and night. The poor man looked so pleased when he brought up poor " Hira " to the door of the Residency and showed me that he was all safe. I am sure I was not the less pleased to see him.

Yesterday, Sunday, there was a report that the city was going to rise, numbers of people having been seen assembling together. About one o'clock the Residency was filled with all the ladies from Mr. Gubbins's, Ommanney's, and Fayrer's. They all assembled in the large room, where luncheon was prepared for them. Such a scene of confusion, talking, and rushing about, first for one thing and then for another, I never witnessed. The alarm turned out a false one. Most of the ladies returned to the different houses where they had been previously located, but some remained in the Residency, Mrs. Inglis among the number, and we arranged to give her and the three children part of our room, as well as Mrs. Giddings; so that the accommodation of our party in that small space was very limited.

CHAP. II.

Tuesday, 9th.

THE heat is very great indeed.   Mrs. Inglis, the children, and Caroline, always sleep on the roof of the house, and as soon as I awake in the morning I go up there, and we have our " chota hagree" brought to us, as it is so much cooler than below till the sun rises. The view from the top of the Residency is truly beyond description beautiful, and in the early morning, when the sun begins to shine on the gilded mosques, and minarets, and towers, it is like a fairy scene.   The whole of this vast city spread out before one, and on all sides surrounded by beautiful parks and magnificent trees, forms a panorama

which it would be difficult to see equalled in
any other part of the world.

We now form a little mess of our own,
Mrs. Inglis having the management of it,
and we are, in consequence, much more comfortable. Mrs. Boileau, Mrs. Radcliffe, and
their children, join us, so that we sit down
to dinner a party of twelve. I always long
for four o'clock, when the messenger arrives
every day with a letter from the camp for
me. I write without fail every night to
William ; Agaib, the bearer, coming in for
my letter before I am awake in the morning.
He always finds it ready on the table, and
the messenger starts with it before daylight,
returning with one for me at four P.M. I
am not so fortunate as the other ladies, who
often have a visit from their husbands ; but
William does not like to leave the camp even
for half-an-hour, so I very seldom see him.
He is now in command of the regiment,

Sir Henry Lawrence having appointed
Colonel Inglis, Brigadier. They are busy
working at our batteries and intrenchments,
and every thing is being done to strengthen
our position. Sir H. Lawrence is inde-
fatigable, and tires out all his staff, who, I
believe, have to take it by turns to go out
with him. It is perfectly wonderful to see
his activity. He never seems to take any
rest, night or day, and appears to live in
his saddle.

The noise of the children in this house is
something dreadful, and there is not one
hole or corner where one can enjoy an instant's privacy. The coming and going, the
talking, the bustle, and noise, inside as well
as outside, the constant alarming reports, and
at times the depressed expression on some
of the countenances, baffle all description.
Dr. Ogilvie says, that where there are so many
people in one house, the hot air is better than
none, consequently all the doors and windows

are wide open, and often the scorching wind which blows in while we are taking our meals in the large room is almost unbearable. Our evenings are usually spent on the top of the house, and sometimes Mrs. Inglis, Carry, and I go down into the Ty Khana, and see the women of the regiment, and any other poor creatures who may have been brought in there from different stations in the district. Mrs. Inglis never goes down empty-handed. She is kind and considerate to every one, and often takes down some pudding or soup, which may have been at dinner, to a poor sick boy. A little tea, sugar, or any old clothes we can find to take with us to them is always very gratefully received, and it cheers their spirits to talk to them a little. Mr. Polehampton reads prayers to us in Mrs. Ogilvie's room at half-past nine, and then we retire for the night, and the sentry's call of " All's well " is generally the last sound I hear before I go to sleep.

Monday, 15th June.

WE continue to suffer a good deal from the heat. Constant reports of murders and horrors in the district are brought in every day, and fugitives who have made their escape from the different places continue to arrive; some come disguised in native dresses. The fall of Delhi is the one great event which we are all longing to hear of. Captain Orr has received a letter from his brother, giving a very sad account of the Shahjihanpore affair. I believe there were twenty-eight of them who reached Mohumdee in safety, only to be murdered afterwards, at Mithowly, in the most barbarous manner. Captain Orr, his wife, and child were saved, and are living in the jungle, exposed to the most dreadful heat and privations of every kind. We are very anxious indeed about the state of things, and the prospect before us is most alarming and gloomy. God in His mercy grant that help for us may be near at hand!

City Residency, Lucknow,
Oct. 30, 1857.

My dearest Gabrielle,

How I long for the moment when I shall be able to send you a letter, feeling sure of its reaching you safely; but still more do I long for the time that, should it please God to spare us, will see us once more together. It is now nearly six months since I have been able to send you one line, and I cannot bear to think of the anxiety you must all be in about us. I shall endeavour to make this a sort of little journal between you

c

and me, which when we meet we may read over together.

At present there is not much to relate; but I will go back to the month of May, and give you as good an account as I can of our doings since that time. They are trying to send out Colonel Inglis's despatch, which I have no doubt you will see in the papers, and a true and clear account it gives of the siege. I shall begin from the day we left our comfortable bungalows, which was on the 17th of May.

As for some time previous to this date there was cause for anxiety lest the 13th, 71st, and 48th Native Infantry, quartered in cantonments about half-an-hour's drive from the city, should mutiny, it was thought advisable to remove the 32nd Regiment from the city, and encamp it somewhere near the lines of the native regiments. Sir Henry Lawrence, then chief commissioner,

invited Mrs. Inglis, ourselves, and Mrs.
Giddings, the paymaster's wife, to his house,
the Residency in cantonments. The Residency in the city was occupied by a party
of the 32nd Regiment and two guns; and
the ladies, wives of the civilians and others,
also took up their abode at Messrs. Ommanney's, Fayrer's, and Gubbins's, whose
houses were all within a short distance of it.

I think you must have received my last
letter, written from our bungalow, when I
told you of a disturbance which took place on
one of the first Sundays in May. Adelaide and
I were going to church at six P.M., and as we
were entering the church an artillery officer,
Mr. Cunliffe, rode up and asked for Colonel
Inglis, who had not yet arrived. As neither
he nor Colonel Case came, we were sure
there was something wrong. As the service
began a large bird, the size of an owl, hovered
over our heads in a melancholy way. As we

drove away from the church, we were met by three of our servants, Azail the shepherd, and Adelaide's syce, who thought we should perhaps find it difficult to get through the city. The 7th Oude Irregular Infantry, stationed at Moosabagh, eight miles off, had mutinied. We met some of the 32nd Regiment, or I should say *all*, going. We found Mrs. Inglis, and Mr. and Mrs. Giddings anxiously waiting in the road for us. Our bungalows were all close to each other; Adelaide's good ayah was in a dreadful state about us, and we all felt very uncomfortable. There was some fear that the city might rise, and we were left with only a guard of the 32nd Regiment at Mr. Giddings's. Adelaide and I took our dinner to Mrs. Inglis's, and spent the evening with her.

After dinner we went to the top of the house. A more beautiful, clear evening, I never saw. The stillness all round was such as I shall never forget. Getting fidgetty to hear some news, we strolled towards Mrs. Giddings's about eleven, and met Major Banks coming from the house. He kindly came to tell us that all had ended quietly. The sepoys, as soon as they saw our guns placed in position, ran away. Great was our delight when William on " Hira " made his appearance soon after ; and we went home and gave him some supper. Adelaide was completely knocked up, and was obliged to go to bed.

The rising of the troops at Meerut, and the horrors committed there, hastened our move. On Saturday the 16th, we had to pack up everything but the furniture. We were occupied till one o'clock, only interrupted by dinner. Poor Adelaide was sadly knocked up. We were to be ready to mount our horses at three o'clock, so I got only an hour's rest, — I cannot say sleep, for I was so restless and hot, that for the first time

I called for my punkah Coolie. At two I jumped up and dressed hastily. Adelaide was very nervous, having heard that we should perhaps be attacked on entering the cantonments. William had gone to see that the 32nd were preparing, and we were to wait until he came back.

About three o'clock, or a little after, we mounted, a most beautiful clear moon shining. Mrs. Inglis lent me her bay pony, "Lalla" having been lame for some time. The carriage was ready for the ayah. There was a great hurry to get our things put into the hackeries. Mrs. Inglis joining us, we agreed to go a little on the road, where were assembled the carriage, with Mrs. Inglis's children, Johnny, Charley, and Alfred the baby; and her buggy with one of the ayahs. Here we waited nearly an hour on our horses, and had just returned to Mrs. Inglis's bungalow to quench our thirst with a glass of iced water, when

William came for us, and we trotted up as fast as we could to our escort, which consisted of a body of mounted sepoys and the 32nd.

We arrived at the Residency at half-past five or six o'clock A.M.   Never was I so thirsty.   I could scarcely speak, my mouth was so parched and dry.   It was a long Sunday, and we were all very tired.   The 32nd encamped on a very good piece of ground in front of the 13th, 71st, and 48th native lines.   The unsettled feeling experienced during the week was very unpleasant. We drove out every evening, but there was no variety.   There was always a large party at dinner.

On Tuesday, the 19th, we were much alarmed at a report that the 71st Native Infantry were going to rise, and also the city at two o'clock.   Carriages were arriving every minute full of ladies and children, ayahs and servants hastening after them with any small bundles they could lay hold of. The house was soon full; but the report ended in nothing, and many of the ladies returned to their bunga-lows. Among the ladies who remained were Mrs. Gall, Mrs. Barber, Mrs. Radclyffe, Mrs. Boileau, Mrs. Hayes, and some others. We used often to drive to the camp, and spend the pleasantest part of our day with William. He generally came to dinner. The next alarm we had was a fire, which broke out somewhere behind the Residency, evidently the work of an incendiary; but it was soon put out.

On Sunday, the 24th, we were at church ; the prayers were not quite over, when we heard one shot and then another. Two officers went out, but returned immediately, and Sir Henry Lawrence not moving re-assured us, but I felt rather alarmed at the thought of going out. At last we recollected that it was the new moon, and it is the custom of the natives to fire when they get the first sight of it.   On Monday I was awoke very early by Adelaide, saying that we must get up immediately to go to the Residency in the city.   The news from Cawnpore was not favourable, and everything seemed in a very uncomfortable, uncertain state.   Accordingly we dressed in haste, leaving the good ayah to pack up all we left behind, and every one drove away quietly as soon as they became aware that they were to do so.*

* The following account of my faithful ayah's wonderful escapes was sent to me, after I arrived at Calcutta, by Mrs. Inglis, and it is so interesting that I quote her letter :—

[handwritten marginal note: Letter from Mrs. Inglis]

"Allahabad, 31st December, 1857.

"Fancy my surprise, two evenings after you left, on returning from our walk to find your ayah and her family had arrived.   Poor woman, she made double marches all the way from Cawnpore, in the hope of seeing you again, and was almost heartbroken when she found that she was disappointed in

We were fortunate to be among the first, for the difficulty of finding rooms was great.

the object of her journey. Had you remained at Benares, she would have followed you I am sure, and even now would go down with me to Calcutta, on the chance of seeing you, but this I dissuaded her from, for it would only be a momentary pleasure to you both, and she would find herself very lonely and friendless when we had all sailed. I have had some very long conversations with her, and the information she gives is most interesting. Upon leaving the Residency, that sad 30th June, she went immediately to our houses, but had not been there half-an-hour before the place was filled with budmashes, and city people, who ransacked the houses, cut up our gardens, &c., &c. Most of our servants ran away, but the metah's children, who hid in a hole, in *our* garden, and covered themselves with manure, where they remained concealed till all the wretches had gone away, and at twelve o'clock at night got out by a hole in the wall, and made towards a village some miles from the city, where they were taken prisoners, brought back to Lucknow, and put in jail. They were kept for a week fed on grain. The king, a boy of about ten years old, came to see them with his mother. They told him that they were not gentlemen's servants, but only poor villagers, and, as

We first drove to Mrs. Gubbins's, where
Mrs. Inglis was.   Mrs. Gubbins offered to

they were almost naked, having been plundered of
everything, he believed their story, and set them free.
They then went to the same village again, and lived
for some months in the jungle, begging for their food,
and hearing daily that the Bailie-guard was to be
taken immediately, and every one killed.   The poor
woman says that she used to dig a hole and hide her
face in it all day, and pray to God to protect you,
whilst her husband and my ayah's used to disguise
themselves and go into Lucknow, to obtain information.   When General Havelock's force arrived they
again made an attempt to enter the Residency, but
were seized by our own soldiers, and accused of being
rebels; but your ayah, by speaking English, and
giving the names of nearly all the officers of the 32nd
Regiment, proved their innocence, and obtained
their release.   They again hid themselves, and when
the Commander-in-Chief's force came, made their
way to cantonments, there they remained, till they
heard that we had all made our retreat.   By a round-
about way they came to Cawnpore.   It was a sad
disappointment to your poor ayah to find you had
left Cawnpore, and she soon started for this place,
where, as I have told you, she arrived two days
too late to see you.   Your dog 'Dandy,' is looking

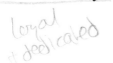

do what she could for us, if we could manage to find room. Mrs. Inglis's room was, however, much too small to take Adelaide and me in, so we went to the Residency, accompanied by Mrs. Edmonstone of the 32nd, where we saw Mrs. Ogilvie, a lady we knew a little of before. She and her husband, Dr. Ogilvie, at first told us that they had no rooms to spare; but whilst we were looking at some rooms downstairs she sent us word to come up, and then offered us one of her own rooms, if we would not mind the servant passing through to get the iced water: I suppose he came through more than thirty times a-day. Of course

very well: he is, just now, my constant companion. I consider their having kept him in good condition speaks volumes for their faithfulness and attachment to you; for having a dog of that description naturally brought suspicion on them. They are good people, and I only trust that they will get good places, for they deserve to be happy."

we did not refuse her kind offer, thinking
ourselves fortunate in getting even a corner
to *ourselves*. So we set to work to clear
it out, and the rest of our things coming
up with the ayah, we soon made ourselves
tolerably comfortable; and in a day or two
a punkah was put up for us. Nothing could
exceed the kindness of Dr. and Mrs. Ogilvie
to us. For a time we joined their little
dinner-party. Every thing went on quietly
till the 30th. Mrs. Inglis used to come
over and see us, and we would drive over
into cantonments, where we always found
the half hour spent there too short.

On the evening of the 30th, Saturday,
just as every one was retiring for the night,
guns were heard, and the gentlemen armed
themselves, and immediately disappeared,
leaving us very anxious. We went out on
one of the verandahs, and there we distinctly
heard the firing, and saw one bungalow

after another set on fire. The stillness in
the city was remarkable; not a sound was
to be heard. It was awful to see the
houses burning. About eleven, or half-past,
the firing diminished, and a message came
from Sir Henry Lawrence to say that it was
nearly over; and we went back to our rooms.
Adelaide and I took in Mrs. Boileau and
her little boy, who had come over, with some
other ladies, from Mrs. Gubbins's and Mrs.
Ommanney's. Most of them returned.
Anxiously did we wait till day dawned.

The usual messenger from the camp
brought Adelaide a note from William,
telling her the occurrences of the previous
night. The sepoys had mutinied. They
attempted to get hold of their officers, but
failed. They then set fire to the bungalows, and plundered them. Lieutenant Grant,
of the 71st Native Infantry, was betrayed
and cruelly murdered, receiving many wounds.

A careless shot, from one of our own guns, *Caroline* went through William's tent, and killed my horse "Lalla" and the old "Sahib." I could not help crying over my poor horse "Lalla." Many a ride have I enjoyed on him, and he brings back to my mind many a pleasant moment. Now I do not regret that he is gone. Brigadier Hanscombe was killed as he went up to harangue the native regiments.

CHAP. III.

On Sunday there was a report that the city was going to rise, numbers of the people being seen assembling together. At one o'clock the house was soon full of people from Mr. Gubbins's, Mr. Ommanney's, and Mr. Fayrer's. They generally assembled in the large room next to ours, and lunch was prepared for them. Such talking, and such rushing about for this and that, I never heard. The alarm ended in nothing, and some of the ladies returned to their friends, but many remained. An old lady, Mrs. Halford, the wife of the Colonel of the 71st (since dead), and her daughter were glad to come to our room for a little quiet. The poor old lady seemed so upset, that we persuaded them to remain the night, which they did, and went back to the Fayrers next morning. Mrs. Inglis, with her three children, had come over, and we arranged to give her part of our room. From this, Sunday night, she and I, and the children, always slept on the roof of the house.

I shall never forget the beautiful moonlight nights and lovely mornings here! The view of the city all round was lovely. Adelaide and Mrs. Giddings, who also shared our room, used to come up and have their cup of tea; and then, when the sun began to be hot, I used, very unwillingly, to go down and dress. The heat was great, quite parching; and we often went to the ice-box for water. There were a number of children in the house, and a famous noise they made. They, the servants, and coprawallahs, about the two large rooms, formed a curious scene. Mrs. Ogilvie, Mrs. Martyn, Mrs. Polehampton, Mrs. Gall,

Mrs. Barber, Mrs. Thornhill, Mrs. Radclyffe, Mrs. Boileau, Mrs. Orr, and Mrs.
Anderson, all lived on the same floor that
we did, and we saw them every day.

The days were sometimes dreadfully long.
We spent our evenings on the top of the
house.   Everything was being done to
strengthen our position; houses knocked
down, batteries made, and trenches, &c. We
used to see Sir Henry Lawrence go out to
inspect the works every morning.   The
troops at Cawnpore mutinied soon after those
here; and Sir Henry had two or three ap-
plications for help from Sir Hugh Wheler,
but our force was too small to spare a man;
and besides, there was no means of sending
them across the river to Cawnpore, the insurgents having destroyed the bridge.

Sir Hugh Wheler and his little force held
out twenty-one days, when, being no longer
able to do so, they came to terms with Nana

Sahib, who promised to let them go to Allahabad in boats: but what did the cowardly
wretch do? They had no sooner got down
to the boats, all had not embarked, when *(Cawnpore now)*
he opened fire upon them! Two of the
boats were sunk; and all the ladies and those
who were not drowned in them were taken
and shut up for a fortnight, when, just as
the troops under General Havelock arrived
at Cawnpore, the very night before they
got in, these savages murdered their prisoners in the most cold-blooded, cruel manner. Poor Mrs. Moore, whose husband,
Captain Moore of the 32nd, was in command
of the party of the 32nd there, was among
the victims. Many died during the siege,
and their sufferings must have been dreadful,
more than we can even imagine. We have
seen Mrs. Moore's servant. His account
was truly sad, and made one's heart ache for
the poor sufferers. They endured great hard-

ships; their food consisted only of dhal and rice, and of that not enough. Only one or two officers escaped. Captain Barrow, of the 90th (Queen's), told us that it was wonderful how they held out so long as they did. And so, my dear Gabrielle, the month of June passed in great anxiety, from the several reports that the enemy were every day getting nearer to us. At night we used to see large fires in all directions, which were no doubt generally signals.

After the rising at Cawnpore, it was difficult to hold communication with any place. Delhi was in the hands of the insurgents, who had murdered every European in the place. All hopes lay in this city being retaken. It was thought that this would have great influence, and prevent an attack upon Lucknow. It has, however, only fallen a little more than a month ago, since the arrival of General Havelock's force at

Cawnpore. The month of June ended very sadly, and the 30th of June threw Adelaide into the greatest grief, for she that morning had to mourn the loss of him who had made her so happy for five years. Colonel Case was killed in the disastrous action at Chinhut, of which by-and-bye. It is indeed a heavy trial for her. You should have lived with him to know his many good and noble qualities. I mourn for him as for a very dear brother. I miss his cheerful face and merry laugh, and if I miss him, what must it be to dear Adelaide. The army, too, has lost in him a brave and gallant officer. He had a warm heart and a fine temper. He was beloved by all who knew him, and his servants, whom he had all the time he was in India, were much attached to him, and have proved themselves faithful by remaining with us now. He never missed a day, while in cantonments, writing to Adelaide, and she to him. He could seldom get away from camp, but when he did, he would come early in the morning; and how he cheered us up! I will insert here one of his notes, to show you how he always encouraged us :—

" Who would have thought we should have been within four miles of each other, and yet not see each other for a week? and I fancy that I am the only one who has not been down, but I dare not leave even for a few minutes. Still I live in hopes that ere long I shall be able to pay you a visit. Truly these are sad times, and I think no nation was ever in such a fix as we are in just now; but don't despair, you'll see we will pull through with the Almighty's aid. The Psalms of this morning ought to give you every encouragement. I derive much every morning from one verse or another that I read, so applicable to our present

condition. You know I have never been
down-spirited about affairs, for I feel that no
cause like that of the mutineers, supported
by murder, fire, and every thing that is savage
and inhuman, will be allowed long to prosper.
There must, and of course will, be many
victories before we get the ascendancy again,
but cheer up, look to the bright side of the
picture, that will, I trust, ere long, be turned
towards us, and pray that success may attend
the endeavours of the loyal to restore peace
and tranquillity to this land, now torn asunder
by sedition and insurrection.

" I don't know who could have seen me do
anything, as what I have done; but if I am
cool and collected, darling, it is because my
prayers to be so under all difficulties and
dangers are answered, and I trust, finally,
my other prayers will be heard too, and that
we may all be preserved to talk over the
past."

Such, my dear Gabrielle, were his cheering notes, which we used to look forward to with such pleasure.

On the 29th of June, the enemy having approached, it was said, within ten miles, William was ordered to strike the camp, and to bring the regiment into the Fort Muchee Bhawun, since blown up. That evening he came to see us as cheerful as ever. Mrs. Inglis was laid up with the small-pox. He had to pass through the room to come to the verandah where we sometimes sat; and as he said good bye to her on his way out he said, " I hope we may meet under happier circumstances."

I slept that night on the verandah, but could not rest for a long time, and often got up to look round me; one of those large birds I mentioned in the beginning kept hovering over my head backwards and forwards, and went several times into our room. I am not superstitious, but this bird made me feel uneasy. In the morning I was awoke very early by Adelaide, who came out on the verandah, looking anxious, and saying that there was something going on. The whole place was astir, cavalry outside the gate, guns going out, and an 8-inch howitzer drawn by elephants, and some of the 32nd. We all dressed as fast as we could, and Adelaide went to see if she could get any news. All she could hear was that a force had been sent out against the enemy. Alas! it was a most wretched day. When they got some miles out, Sir Henry Lawrence sent to reconnoitre, and the party returned without seeing any thing of the enemy. Sir Henry was on the point of returning to the city, but, unfortunately, he was persuaded to advance, as it was said the enemy could not be in great number. So the order was given, but when they came in

sight of the mutineers, they proved to be
very strong, 12,000 men, it was said. They
closed in upon our little force; our native
artillerymen ran their guns into nullahs and
cut the traces of the horses and elephants.
The howitzer fell into the enemy's hands.
Desperate efforts were made to get it back,
but the enemy's force was overwhelming
and it was relinquished. William was shot
through the heart whilst rallying his men.
How one returned to tell the tale is a marvel.
They came in one by one as they best could,
looking more dead than alive. Poor Adelaide
and Mrs. Inglis stood at a window watching
the sad scene.

At nine o'clock Colonel Inglis got back,
and then it was that poor Adelaide heard the
sad news. She had no time, poor thing, to
give way to her grief. Not a moment was
to be lost in leaving our room for a safer
place, and we had to hurry and put up our

things. Oh, what a scene it was! Every
one had left before we had. Poor Mrs.
Inglis, still very ill with the small-pox. We
got down as far as where the artillery soldiers and their wives lived, and had to spend
the day there. The firing was so great we
could not get to any other place of shelter
till evening. It was very close and hot.
The poor soldiers came running in for a
glass of water, and we had to barricade the
windows on account of the bullets.

When the firing diminished a little in the
evening, we managed to get across to the
room Colonel Inglis had been arranging for
himself. It was about ten minutes' walk from
the Residency House, in a square surrounded
by other enclosures, and the walls being high
it was considered to be about the safest place.
The room is just large enough to contain us
three ladies and the three children. It is a
most bare-looking place. Colonel Inglis had

the place whitewashed.   It looks like a room
where provisions or something of the kind
had been kept.   We have a bath-room, where
the grain for the goats is kept.   Shortly after
the siege began, Sir Henry was struck in the
leg by a shot from that very howitzer we
lost at Chinhut.   He was sitting writing at
the time, and only survived two days.   He
was deeply regretted by the garrison, and
was a very great loss as an artillery officer.
Major Banks succeeded, but was killed by a
round shot at Mr. Gubbins's.   Since his
death Colonel Inglis (Brigadier) has had
the entire command of the garrison.

I cannot give an account of each of the
different attacks of the enemy.   At first
the fire was continual, night and day.   To
give you an idea how incessant it was, I
must tell you, that when it ceased we quite
missed it, and felt almost uncomfortable.   Of
course, I do not mean to say that when it did

cease, after a time, it was not a great re-
prieve. The mutineers would then commence
at different times, leaving you some days
tolerably quiet.   They would suddenly commence a heavy musketry firing, which might
last about an hour or so ; and how glad we
were when we heard our guns firing away
upon them. We soon learnt to distinguish our
guns from theirs.   We have destroyed seven
or eight of their mines.   They never made a
real attack ; they were never bold enough, after
the first commencement, to push their way on.
These night attacks, for they were most generally in the night, and the mines, were very
harassing to the men ; then the rains came on,
and they had to undergo the extreme changes
between heat and cold, but they kept their
health better than might be expected under
the circumstances. Casualties occurred daily ;
not in the heaviest firing, when we expected
to hear of many being hit, but by stray shots

during the day. A mine of the enemy's killed seven of our drummers. We lost nearly every good officer before the arrival of reinforcements, particularly among the Engineers.

Great was our anxiety to hear of troops coming to our relief; it was most difficult to send any message out. The letters were sent in a small quill about an inch long, which I believe they hid in their mouth, hair, or ears.

CHAP. IV.

ON the 26th July, a messenger came in
with a letter from Colonel Tytler, Quarter-
master-general, saying that two thirds of the
force marching to our relief had crossed
the river ; that they had beaten the Nana
Sahib, and his army had dispersed nobody
knew where. Bithoor was in our possession,
and they hoped to be in Lucknow in five or
six days. The messenger went out again the
same evening with an answer and a plan of the
city, and he is to get 500*l.* if he delivers
it safe. On the 16th of August, another
letter arrived from Colonel Tytler, dated
the 4th, saying they were on their way
to Lucknow, but the messenger had later

news, and told us they had had another engagement with the enemy, who were beaten
with great loss. The relieving army had,
however, returned to Cawnpore, to wait for
the China force, which was coming out from
England.

On the 29th August (last night) a messenger came in from Cawnpore with a letter
from General Havelock to Colonel Inglis,
as follows : —

                        " Cawnpore, Aug. 24, 1857.

    " MY DEAR COLONEL,

          " I have your letter of the 16th
inst.   I can only say hold on, and do not
negotiate, but rather perish sword in hand.
Sir Colin Campbell, who came out at a day's
notice to command, upon the news arriving
of General Anson's death, promises me fresh
troops, and you will be my first care.   The
reinforcements may reach me in from twenty

to twenty-five days, and I will prepare every thing for a march on Lucknow.

"Yours sincerely,

"H. HAVELOCK, M.-General."

This was disheartening news to hear the first thing in the morning: however, any thing is better than their coming on with too small a force. The messenger told us that the Nana at Cawnpore had been twice beaten by our troops, but that fifty Europeans had been killed by falling into an ambush of the 42nd N. I. He added that the insurgents round us are about 11,000, that they have a council of war every day, and every day order an attack. On Wednesday, Sept. 23rd, arrived a letter from General Outram, dated 20th September.

On Friday the 25th Sept. the long looked for reinforcement came in. At 12 P.M. they entered the city. They had a hard fight to

get through the narrow streets, the enemy
inside the houses firing down on them, and
the loss was very severe.   At 6 p.m. great
was the excitement inside the garrison, and
great the cheering.   Some of the troops
had arrived, — the 78th Highlanders, the
1st Madras Fusileers, and some artillery and
Sikhs.   We hear that the loss coming in
was between 500 and 600.   The 90th Regiment did not come in until the next day,
when they had a great deal of difficulty
in making their way, they were so encum-
bered with baggage and ammunition.   Every
available man in the garrison, and the 32nd,
were sent to their assistance.

General Havelock dined with us on the
26th, and there was much discussion as to
future operations.   At one time it was almost
feared it would be necessary to abandon
the guns, which were impeding the progress
of that part of the 90th coming in, rather

than sacrifice so many lives, now so valuable. All felt our force was not equal to the emergency. Never shall I forget the scene that day. We dined in a very large room, if you can call it a room at all; the walls were not even white-washed, and there was no matting or any thing to cover the ground. The only light came through the large door, and near this we placed the table. The goats were kept at one end at night, and the other end was filled with Colonel Inglis's boxes. The confusion baffles description. The day General Havelock dined with us poor Colonel Campbell, 90th Regiment, lay wounded, a very little distance from the table.

Sunday, 27th.

EVERY one was to-day out of spirits; in fact, we felt we were not relieved, but only reinforced.   A party, consisting of one hundred men, and eighteen of the 32nd, commanded by Captain Warner, went out to try and get some of the enemy's guns.   The guns were not taken, but two were spiked. The portion of the 90th left behind with the baggage did not come in.   They have intrenched themselves about four miles outside the city in a very good position, at a place called Alumbagh, and are doing very well and receiving reinforcements.

I felt more depressed on Monday the 28th than I had done since I have been shut up, but Hope soon rose again, and I cannot feel long desponding.   We must put our trust in Him who has protected us so long; and although we have undergone much discomfort, we have much to be thankful for.   Till the relieving force came in, we were not reduced in our rations; it is only now we are. Colonel Inglis had got in some supplies of his own, and with Mrs. Inglis's good management, I think that we shall not starve. Sugar and arrowroot have for some time past come almost to an end, but we still manage to have enough for the children. I cannot bring myself to drink tea without sugar, so I am treated as one of the children, and restrict myself to one cup a day at breakfast, and get a bit of sugar for it.　We have now no soap, and no Dhoby, so I wash Adele's and my things, and it is rather hard work.　One morning I swept the room, the ayah being very busy with her boy, who was ill of pleurisy. The dust is dreadful, and though the room is swept twice every day, it is impossible to get rid of it.　I dislike the half hour before dinner, particularly if it is at four o'clock, for just as one is *en train* for work, in comes the ayah with her broom, and we are driven out into the square, and even there you are pursued by the dust.　Mosquitoes abound, and on account of them we are obliged to have the punkah at night, otherwise we should be cool enough without it. The moonlight nights are beautiful ; so bright, it makes one long to be outside.

On the 29th September a party went out to take some of the enemy's guns, which was composed of men from the different regiments. They started at five o'clock in the morning, and, as usual, the brave 32nd leading, Mr. M'Cabe of that regiment having the command. This was his fourth sortie; and his last, for he was mortally wounded; he was a very good officer, and got his commission for bravery, having risen from the ranks. The party returned about ten, having taken seven guns, most of which had been previously spiked by the 32nd. On the night of the 30th Captain Harding, a very brave officer, made an attempt to go to Alumbagh with some of his Sikhs, but did not get far, the enemy's fire being too heavy upon them. The morning they went out to take the guns two men fell into a well; one of them was killed, but the other, belonging to the 32nd, escaped unhurt. He was three days in the well, not daring to call out till he heard European voices.

On Saturday, 3rd October, guns were heard in the direction of Alumbagh. They have there (at least then they had, for they have since been reinforced) 250 fighting men, and they have enough provisions to last some time. Sugar is not to be got now here, 25 rupees (2*l.* 10*s.*) were offered for two pounds, but in vain. Mrs. Inglis paid two rupees (4*s.*) for a very small piece of soap. You must pay a good price for any thing you want to buy, if indeed it is to be got at all. Beer and porter are finished. I have made this letter very long! Oh! I wish I could get as long a one from you, it would be such a treat.   I am sure there are some letters from you among those left behind at Alumbagh, and I should bear my captivity better if I could know that you knew something of us, for you must be so anxious.

Yours, &c.

City Residency, Lucknow,
Friday, 6th November, 1857.

MY DEAREST GABRIELLE,

In my last letter to you, I brought up my long account of ourselves to the 1st November.   I shall, however, in this, have to tell you some things which I forgot.   I did not tell you that dear Adelaide was laid up for more than a week in July, and was very, very weak for two or three days.   On the 20th of July I took the small pox, and was in bed for ten days. It was fortunately slight, and has left no traces. One lady, wife to Captain Thomas, Madras Artillery, and also some children, died of this disease, but most of the cases were slight. We have been living upon beef and rice for the last four months; no vegetables. Now we do get occasionally some green herb resembling spinach, and a great treat it is. I like the rice, which I don't tire of. The meat, with the exception of two or three times, has been good and tender. I hear people, however, complaining very much about it. This last week we have had some mutton. Our substitute for bread is chupatties, upon which the natives live. Since we have had reduced rations, and learnt that we must spin out our provisions to the 1st December, we have restricted ourselves to a certain number a day. We have enough to eat, and it is wonderful how long the provisions have lasted, particularly when one

thinks of the addition the new force made to
our numbers. We owe it all to the good
management of the Commissariat Officer,
Captain James. It is quite wonderful to
think how well our provisions hold out.
How deeply indebted we are, under Providence, to Captain James, for his judicious
management of all the stores at the commencement of the siege ! It must have
been very difficult *at first* to be careful, and
required no common foresight to accom-
plish this so admirably. For our own rations we used at first to get rice, tea, attah,
sugar, coffee, salt, and pepper. Now we get
all but tea, sugar, and coffee. But we
have plenty of tea of our own, and a little
sugar. Mrs. Inglis says, that having to deal
out things so sparingly makes her feel very
miserly. She manages very well indeed. It
will be a perfect luxury to feel clean again,
for the dust is so great that it is really almost

useless to dust any thing in our room. We are overrun with rats and mice.

I cannot tell you of all the casualties which have occurred in the garrison since the commencement of the siege, but I may mention two; first, Miss Palmer, whose leg was carried off by a round shot the first day of the siege, and she died. She was only twenty, and must be a sad loss to her poor father, Colonel Palmer. The other was Mr. Polehampton, the clergyman, whom we liked very much. He was first badly wounded, and afterwards died of cholera. We felt much for his poor wife. The children have suffered greatly, and many have died. There was very little milk to be had for them. Mrs. Inglis fortunately had her goats inside. Her children, Johnny, Charlie, and baby, have kept, on the whole, very well, though they have had their share of sickness, in the way of fevers and bad colds. The nights and

mornings are now cold ; but we are obliged to have the punkahs on account of
the musquitoes.   The days are very warm.
They have not been able to send off the
despatch yet.

In the beginning of October General Sir
James Outram published a most flattering
order about the manner in which the garrison
has been defended by Colonel Inglis and the
officers and men under his command.   The
whole affair he describes as being unparalleled
in the annals of history.   The troops at Alumbagh have been reinforced, and Sir Colin
Campbell, the Commander-in-chief, was expected at Cawnpore yesterday.   Report says
he is on this side of the river.   The force
from Delhi, under Colonel Grant of the 9th
Lancers, is also close to Alumbagh.

Our army had hard work to take Delhi :
and our loss was severe.   Sixty-one officers
and 2000 men killed and wounded.   I hope

that they will come up in sufficient strength this time, and that we shall be able really to get away. Since the arrival of Generals Outram and Havelock we have had very little firing. Once or twice at night there has been some sharp musketry, but all on the enemy's side. We have just had a visit from Major Eyre of the Artillery, who came with the reinforcement.

Wednesday, 11th.

ON Friday night a messenger came in with a letter from Cawnpore, from Major Bruce, stating that the force commanded by Sir Colin Campbell in person was expected to reach Alumbagh on the 10th (yesterday). It consists of 5100 infantry and 600 cavalry, and thirty-six guns. A salvo was to be fired at two o'clock yesterday, if they arrived. In the morning heavy guns were heard at Alumbagh : and they are expected to be here on the 15th. I trust they will not suffer so much as General Havelock's troops.

Our exit will of course depend much upon Sir Colin Campbell's success. Should the enemy not be entirely dispersed, we shall be all immediately sent off, and only allowed to take what we require in our hand. And should this be the case, we shall have to leave behind some things we value. This helps to make us regret the things we have lost, for it is more difficult to give up a thing than to lose it. However, I hope we shall get away better than that, and be able to take a box each. I dare say some of us will have to walk, as all the carriages, &c., will be taken up for the sick and wounded. The great difficulty will be getting away from this place. Once at Alumbagh, I hope it will be easier.

Colonel Inglis has not been at all well these three last days, but is better to-day.

When General Havelock's force came in, Colonel Campbell, of the 90th, was wounded, and Colonel Inglis gave him up the large room at the end of our square, in which we sometimes dined. At first he went on very well, and his wound was considered slight, but fever ensued, and the wound in his leg getting worse in consequence, to-day at twelve the sad operation of amputation was performed. Fortunately, they had some chloroform left. He bore it wonderfully, and they say that he is going on well, though very weak.

I am very tired, my pen is bad, and the ink still worse, so I shall conclude.

Deil Cusha Park,
Monday, 23rd November, 1857.

MY DEAR GABRIELLE,

It is now a fortnight since I last wrote to you; I told you that poor Colonel Campbell was very weak. He rapidly sank, and on Thursday night, the 12th, he died. I must tell you a strange circumstance in relation to his illness. A white fowl had been brought to Mrs. Inglis for sale, but she thought the price, five rupees, was much too high. However, Colonel Inglis bought it. Its legs were secured, and it constantly hopped about before our door. Mrs. Inglis thought it was too bad that it should be eating our rice, and was just going to order it to be killed and cooked for dinner, when little Johnny comes running into the room,—"Mamma, Mamma, the white fowl has laid an egg!" This saved its life. Colonel Campbell was very fond of an egg — it was the only thing he could take well. The white fowl from this notable day laid an egg daily till Colonel Campbell died, after which it never laid another. We have brought the fowl away, and, may be, it will some day be in England.

I forgot to say in my last, that Mr. Kavanagh, head clerk in Mr. Cooper's office, volunteered to go out on the 9th inst. to Alumbagh, and conduct Sir Colin Campbell's force into Lucknow. This was a most gallant act on his part, and his safe arrival was announced the next day by hoisting a flag. He went out at night disguised as a native, taking a man with him as guide. He must have proved of great use to the force, as

E

there was no one there who knew any thing of this part of the country.

The enemy made an attack on Alumbagh on the morning of the 12th, but were repulsed with the loss of their guns. On Tuesday, the 13th, sharp musketry firing was heard at Alumbagh. Since General Havelock's force came in on the 25th October, Colonel Inglis had 100 of his own garrison killed and wounded, and twenty-six of the 32nd killed.

Very heavy firing was heard on Saturday the 14th instant, between twelve and one o'clock, and our flag was seen flying from the Martinière College. Sir Colin had got possession of this park (the Deil Cusha) and the Martinière. Sir Colin did not advance on Sunday the 15th, as was expected by the garrison, who were in a great state of excitement, watching every movement. It was a very quiet day with us. We had the

service read in the Brigade Mess-room, close
to our room. On Sunday night at ten o'clock
the enemy commenced a heavy firing upon us,
but it lasted only a short time. I could not
sleep much that night, as I could only listen
to the distant guns I heard. Again, at four
o'clock in the morning, they fired very heavily
upon us. However, I believe it was chiefly
blank ammunition. Sir Colin did not advance farther than Secundra Bagh, a palace
with gardens.

On Tuesday the 17th, Sir Colin advanced
and took possession of the 32nd Messhouse,
and then Mr. Martin's bungalow. This ef-
fected a communication between the garrison
and the force; and in the evening Colonel
Berkeley, the new colonel of the 32nd, rode
into our court-yard to see Colonel Inglis. On
that Tuesday, the 17th, at dinner, Colonel
Inglis told us that Sir Colin's orders were that
the whole force was to leave Lucknow the

next day.   We were perfectly astounded.
How the sick and wounded, women and children, were all to be moved so quickly we could
not imagine. We got up very early on Thursday morning, as we had much to do, and the
hour of our departure was so uncertain.   I
find now that we shall not leave the Residency till the 22nd. I am very busy, and can
say no more at present, and so farewell!

[*End of Miss Dickson's Letters to her
Cousin.*]

CHAP. V.

[Recommencement of Mrs. Case's Journal.]

Sunday, July 5th, 1857.

CAROLINE's letters which precede this will explain to you why I have not been able to write for some time past. Knowing how deeply interested you will be about us, I will endeavour to write down something every day, though I think it very doubtful whether you will see it or receive our letters. This is indeed a truly awful time : death seems ever before us, and I will not attempt to describe our sensations, because it would be impossible to do so, and indeed they could scarcely be understood by those who are enjoying the privilege of peace and quiet by their happy firesides in England. There is so much sorrow and suffering around us, that there is scarcely time to indulge in private grief, but deeply I know you will feel for me.

We are now under a heavy fire from the enemy night and day. Mrs. Inglis and her three children, Carry and myself, are all in a very small room, inside the square, near the brigade mess; but Colonel Inglis considers it safer than most places from the shot and shell, which fall about in all directions. We have two sofas, on one of which I sleep. Mrs. Inglis, Carry, and the children all sleep on mattresses on the floor. In the day time they are rolled up and put away, and we try to make our little room look as neat as we can, for it is used as a drawing-room, as well as for a sleeping apartment. We are, I believe, more comfortable than any other people in the Residency in one respect, for our servants and Mrs. Inglis's have remained with us. As we are four in number, besides the children, our rations go farther than they would do with a smaller party.

It is impossible to tell you how kind Colonel and Mrs. Inglis have been to us. They have insisted on our considering ourselves as part of their family, and in such times as these how doubly valuable are kindness and sympathy?

The firing is incessant night and day. The day after we were first besieged, it appeared to our ears, so unaccustomed to any thing of the kind, to be most awful. We did not know what was going on, and as every man who could carry a musket was at his post, we could get no information, and thought every moment that the place must be taken by storm; and we knew that if the enemy did get in a dreadful fate would have been reserved for us. Mrs. Inglis was ill in bed, just beginning to recover from the small pox. We three offered up our prayers to Him who could alone protect us. I read the Litany aloud, and so wonderful was the effect of that heartfelt prayer, that it is scarcely too much to say, that we rose from our knees calm, and feeling ready for whatever might await us. The great terror which we experienced only a few minutes before seemed to disappear, and fresh strength to have taken its place. I am thankful to say that the enemy were repulsed in that attack.

A very sad event has happened to us ; the death of that good and excellent man, Sir Henry Lawrence. On the 1st July he was hit while sitting in his room by a ball from the very howitzer which the enemy had taken from us at Chinhut. The wound proved mortal, and he died two days afterwards, regretted by the whole garrison. Poor Miss Palmer, the daughter of Colonel Palmer, of the 48th Native Infantry, a young girl of about twenty, had her leg taken off by a round shot entering her room. She died the following day. Some officers and men have been wounded, but, considering that day and night they are under such heavy fire, it is not surprising. Last night the rain fell in torrents, and the thunder and lightning were awful, during which time the firing never ceased. Oh, how glad we were when the first peep of dawn was seen : our courage feels renewed when daylight appears. I hear that the enemy's force round the Residency are in great numbers, and that they have a great many guns ; but our brave little handful of Europeans, scarcely numbering 800, are holding out nobly.

Monday, July 6th.

Last evening there was a rumour among the natives that two regiments were coming in. I believe that there was some fighting going on in the direction of the Dil Koosha: it is supposed to have been among the natives themselves. This is the best thing that can happen for us, as it takes them away from the place. The enemy were very close to us yesterday, and burnt down a tent which had been prepared for Mrs. Inglis, when she was first seized with the small pox. Last night was fine and light, and much quieter than the previous. Colonel Inglis breakfasted with us. Some nights ago the rebels looted the city, and the yelling and screaming were terrific. If they could only effect an entrance here, how dreadful would be our fate! Firing is still going on, but nothing compared to what it was during the past week. The natives in the garrison say that the insurgents are constructing a mine to blow us all up, but we have heard no real information to that effect. How long is all this to last? My

poor heart is so weary and sad, that I feel
truly desolate and lonely now in the world;
and well indeed may I feel so, having lost one
who was truly every thing to me. Weather
fine to-day : no rain. Captain Lowe came in
whilst we were at dinner.

Tuesday, July 7th.

SOME heavy firing during the night. Colonel Inglis came to breakfast. The Light
Company of the regiment assembled in our
square, and went to the top of the house to
fire on the enemy. Officers and men look
both very tired and worn. Day cloudy, close,
and sultry. Major Francis badly wounded.

Wednesday, July 8th.

VERY heavy rain last night; also after breakfast this morning. Firing still continues: very sharp about 1 P.M. Colonel Inglis came in at two o'clock, and told us that Mr. Polehampton had been shot through the body, but he does not know whether the wound is dangerous. I pray it may not be. A shell fell close to our cook-room door, quite near the khansamah, while he was making the soup : he must have had a narrow escape. Major Francis had both his legs shot off, and they say that his recovery is very doubtful. I think and fear that we shall hear of many more sad things before all this dreadful business ends. All at present wears a most dismal aspect. The rain makes every one and every thing look most miserable, and in the trenches it must be dreadful. My poor heart aches. I wonder what has become of my poor Hira? All the horses were turned out of this some days ago. Of course he fell into the hands of the insurgents. What an ending to such a favourite animal, one which had carried me so many happy miles on his back. Carry's Lalla shared a better fate with the poor old Sahib, being shot the first night of the outbreak in camp.

I forgot to mention that on Wednesday the 1st July, the day after we came in here, the Fort Muchee Bhawun was blown up by our own people, and the whole party came in bringing their sick with them; and all, to our surprise, in perfect safety. We heard the explosion: it was very loud. It took place between twelve and one at night. Yesterday a gallant charge was made by some of the 32nd and some Sikhs, about fifty men altogether, into Mr. Johannes' house, a position which the enemy had taken up, and where it was supposed they were mining. This turned out, however, not to be the case; and the brave little party returned with only two men wounded, having killed eight of the enemy. Major and Mrs. Banks came in to see Mrs. Inglis while we were at dinner, and Mr. and Mrs. Turnbull came to talk to her some time.

Thursday, July 9th.

LAST night, or rather early this morning, the firing was very loud indeed, and the rain heavy at times. Heard a report again that the enemy were mining. We hear that they are going to offer Maun Sing five lacs of rupees (5000*l.*) to come and fight on our side, for he is said to be here, but as yet neutral. They purpose sending out six messengers, and they are to get 100*l.* each for carrying the message. I should think it doubtful whether even one will ever reach him. Colonel Inglis brought me yesterday my dear William's Bible, Prayer Book, and a little " Companion to the Altar," which I had given him. It was entirely shot through by a ball. These, with another Prayer Book, were the only things of his saved at the Muchee Bhawun.

Friday, July 10th.

LAST night was quieter than usual ; much less firing. We heard at breakfast there was a report that part of the force which had returned from Persia had arrived at Cawnpore, and would be here very shortly. Day fine but showery. Dr. Boyd came to Mrs. Inglis in the evening while we were sitting outside our door. He told her that he could not find any one to take charge of Mrs. Stephens's little boy while she was ill.   She was confined last night, but the child was born dead.

Saturday, July 11th.

THE night past appeared very quiet to us, but when Colonel Inglis came to breakfast, he told us that he had been called up in the night, for a man had come in with the intelligence that the enemy meant to attack us. It turned out to be a false alarm.   There was, however, I believe, a good deal of firing on the other side of the Residency.   Weather very hot and oppressive to-day.

Sunday, July 12th.

FIRING much as usual during the night. Day fine but very close. Colonel Inglis read the morning service to us after breakfast. How little it appears like Sunday, that day which always used to be such a happy one to me! Heavy firing during the night, chiefly, I believe, from the enemy. There appears to be no news; indeed, nobody knows any thing of what is going on beyond the precincts of this Residency. Surely there never was in the annals of history a more extraordinary state of things than this. When will it all end? The natives say they have heard that our bungalows have been looted, and all the servants who were left there killed. I trust this is not the case, for we cannot help hoping that the poor creatures would be able to get away to some village before these wretches commenced their work of plunder and destruction. How sorry I should be if any thing were to happen to <u>my poor good ayah</u>.

Care for servants & dishnchan between Indian people

Monday, July 13th.

LAST night the firing was very loud indeed, but from what we heard at breakfast there does not appear to have been any thing very particular going on. Day fine, but cloudy. When Colonel Inglis came in to dinner he told us that poor Mr. Charlton (32nd) had been badly wounded by a ball through his head, and that he did not think he would live. Heavy rain just after dinner, which prevented us from sitting outside our door as usual. Mrs. Need spoke to

Mrs. Inglis and told her of some little child which had just died. We saw it carried past in the dark to its last resting place. We saw no Europeans with it, poor little thing! The khansamah told us just before we went to bed that seventeen men, including Europeans and natives, had been wounded, but I know not if it be true.

Tuesday, July 14th.

ABOUT nine o'clock this morning, just as we had finished dressing, there appeared to be a good deal of excitement. It seemed that the insurgents had collected in great numbers, and were intending to make an attack; but finding our force on the look out for them did not then carry out their intentions, whatever they may have been. Mr. Charlton is better to-day, but I fear that

there is but little hope of his life being saved.
The enemy have been trying to annoy us a
good deal.   There was heavy firing just
after our dinner, which must have frightened the ladies, as the verandah of the building where they are was hit.   One of the
officers, who was passing by while we were
sitting outside our door, ordered us to go
in, as it was scarcely safe to sit out while the
balls were flying about in that manner.   We
saw a poor man carried by who had his leg
shot off (one of the 32nd).   Dr. Boyde came
and spoke to Mrs. Inglis for a few minutes
in the evening.   The insurgents tried to
effect a breach in the wall, but were unsuccessful.

Wednesday, July 15th.

LAST night appeared to me very noisy, but it does not seem to have been much more so than usual. While we were dressing, a round shot fell close to our door; most providentially no one happened to be on the spot at the time. A bullet fell close to the khansamah, while he was cooking the breakfast; and one also close to the chick, near which Mrs. Inglis was sitting settling something in one of her boxes. For the first time, to-day the khansamah has complained of being short of wood for cooking. He has, however, found some. If things came to the worst we should have to break up our tables and chairs for fire-wood. Some of the poor ladies fare badly, I believe, in the way of provisions, many having laid in no private stores of their own, and are entirely dependent on their rations, which of course are but scanty. Dr. Scott came to see us. I believe it is only the second time since his illness that he has been out. He looked very weak and broken down, but rather better in face than we expected to see him. I am sure he felt a good deal at seeing me. His recovery is wonderful, after so severe an illness. Dr. Boyde also came in the afternoon. He told us Mr. Charlton is wonderfully well, but I do not think any hope of his recovery is entertained, though Dr. Boyde said he had known an instance of a person recovering with a bullet lodged in the head. Came inside earlier than usual, for Captain Wilson told us as he passed by that it was not safe to remain outside, as they were going to send off a shell.

Thursday, July 16th.

WHEN Colonel Inglis came to see us this morning at our early tea, he told us that his servant (Vokins, a 32nd man) had his leg struck by a round shot yesterday evening, while sitting in a chair under the portico of the hall door at the Residency. The leg was amputated, but the poor man was too weak to have chloroform administered to him, and suffered dreadfully. Colonel Inglis held him while they performed the operation; he is going on as well as he can be expected to do.

To-day is little Johnny's birthday; he is four years old to-day, poor little fellow! It is not a very happy birthday for him. We must only hope that the next one may be in England.

I have been too ill to write for some days, so shall copy here what dear Carry has been kind enough to write for me.

(Gap where Adelaide was too ill to continue)

Friday, July 17th.

ADELAIDE being too ill to continue her journal, I do so for her, till she is well again. She rose yesterday morning with a sore throat, and headache came on in the afternoon. Mrs. Inglis and I persuaded her to lie down, and see Dr. Scott in the evening.

On Thursday night there was a heavy fire of musketry, between eleven and twelve, from the side of the Cawnpore Battery, which lasted about half-an-hour. The guns continued firing all night. None of our people were hit. Yesterday was a very

quiet day, which we paid for at night. Again
at half-past eleven we were startled out of
our sleep by a very heavy and furious firing,
both of musketry and artillery. It was
frightful, and seemed as if it were to be our
last struggle. In half-an-hour it was over,
and the rest of the night was quiet. Mrs.
Inglis says that there was some loud firing
early in the morning, but it was chiefly from
our own guns. It was such a relief to see
Colonel Inglis last night after the firing.
He came to tell us that all was right. Poor
Adelaide, who had taken, when she went
to bed, a composing draught, and had fallen
into a comfortable sleep, was roused by it,
and did not get a good sleep again till after
four o'clock. She was dreadfully weak. In
the night we had to give her port-wine constantly. Several very loud shots are to be
heard. A man of the 32nd was wounded
this morning, and a sergeant of the Artillery

killed. No one hurt in last night's firing.
Colonel Inglis is very kind.   He brings
Adelaide all he thinks will do her good.
I must not forget to mention the escape he
had yesterday morning. He slept in the
Residency, which is a great mark for the
enemy, and had left his room only ten minutes, when a round-shot came through it,
passed over his bed and tub, and through his
portmanteau. He has now removed his quarters elsewhere. Mrs. Inglis had only the day
before been saying, how wrong it was to stop
there.   It was a narrow escape indeed.

When he came into luncheon he told us
there was a man just outside the gate with
a stick in his hand, who had been killed by
either our guns or the enemy's.   They fancy
he might be the bearer of some despatches,
and are going to try and get him in after
dark.

CHAP. VI.

Sunday, 19th July.

AFTER dinner last night, Mrs. Thornhill came to see Mrs. Inglis, and Mr. Thornhill also, and brought the report that the Rajah of Cawnpore had been taken. About half-past eight Colonel Inglis looked in, and said they had got in the body which had lain at the gate; however, it turned out to be an ayah. At twelve last night there was some heavy firing, but nothing like the night before. An officer of the 7th Cavalry (Mr. Arthur) was killed this morning; he exposed himself too much. Mr. Harmer (32nd) had his leg much hurt by the splinter of a round shot which passed through the mess-room while they were at breakfast in the Residency. A carcase came into Colonel Inglis's room there last night, and set fire to part of it. Adelaide had a good night, but still suffers much from her head. At Dr. Fayrer's they have not a room which is safe, and they have no servants left, so they have to do every thing themselves. How I long for all this to be at an end! Mrs. Inglis and I take a walk up and down a very small space. We are perfect prisoners, but are fortunate in being able to get out at all.

Monday, July 20th.

THIS morning, between eight and nine, we heard all the cranies in our square ordered to their posts. An alarm was given that the enemy were going to attack us. This proved true. They assembled in great numbers on the side of the church ; the firing was very heavy for a long time, but they were repulsed. They appeared to be so sure of getting in, that they sent their standard-bearer to place their standard quite close to the gate ; he was immediately shot dead. Mr. Edmonstone was slightly wounded. Firing still continues, but I fancy all is right for this time. The night was a very quiet one. Whilst we were sitting at breakfast, what seemed to us a large gun going off, made the whole ground and building shake. It was a mine which the enemy had blown up close to the intrenchments, as their signal to commence the attack. It fortunately did us no harm. It has been the severest attack we have had, and I am so thankful that it did not take place in the night. We heard yesterday evening that Mr. Polehampton was very ill with cholera, and I fear he can scarcely be alive now. A lady at the Begum's house (Mrs. Thomas) died a few days ago of small-pox. We had met her at Colonel Palmer's when she first came to Lucknow. Two soldiers' children also died of it. The firing of musketry very sharp at this minute. The day is cloudy. The flies here are a perfect plague; one can scarcely eat one's breakfast, dinner, or any thing without being attacked by millions of them. At four P.M. the firing ceased, and the stillness is quite strange. Mr. Cooper has just told Mrs. Inglis that the enemy have been well punished to-day. He says, that they were to be seen going over the bridge, carrying their dead and wounded in carts-full. They heard of the reinforcements for us being near, and were making a desperate attempt to get hold of the treasury and kill us all, and then make off. They also appeared to have received reinforcements; but whether they were regiments which they sent out to intercept the troops coming to our relief, and which report says were between this and Cawnpore, or a fresh body of men, is not known.   At all events, they were seen coming in from the Cawnpore road this morning.   Mr. Healy, the veterinary surgeon, had his arm broken by a stray shot, whilst carrying a message.   At two o'clock we expected another attack would be made.   About twenty men got inside the palisades somewhere on our side, but were driven out.   Only fancy being within only a few hundred yards of creatures, who, if they could but get in, would murder us in the most brutal manner, and commit horrors too fearful even to think of!   God, in his infinite mercy, preserve us from such a fate, and soon send us relief.   Our little garrison is holding out well, and they say we have provisions for a month longer.

[*Caroline ceases here, and Mrs. Case be-gins again.*]

F 4

Tuesday, July 21st.

Poor Carry has not been well for the last
two days, and to-day she is very feverish. *I*
(thank God for all His mercies !) am getting
better, though not very strong ; but am able
to resume my journal again.

Not much firing going on to-day, though
I believe they are constantly expecting something. Poor Major Banks has been killed
this morning. His is a public loss indeed !
He exposed himself too much, and it was
only this morning that Colonel Inglis wrote
to him and told him that he ought to consider how useful and valuable his life was,
and begged him to be more careful. It is
much to be regretted he did not follow this
advice, for when he was killed he was firing,
just as any private soldier, from the top of

Mr. Gubbins's house. He was a most excellent man, and, I believe, a very clever officer. There is no one here qualified to fill his place.

I got up yesterday evening, for a short time, about five o'clock. I never remember in my life to have felt so weak as I did one night while I was ill, and I firmly believe I should not have lived, had not my two kind nurses, Mrs. Inglis and Carry, given me a quantity of port-wine. I feel as if my poor nerves, and indeed my whole frame, were much and severely shaken. The least thing makes me feel as if I should drop down.

Wednesday, July 22nd.

VERY heavy rain this morning till about one, when it cleared up. Dr. Scott came to see us before breakfast. Carry still very unwell. She is very heavy and sleeps a great deal. Very little firing going on to-day. They must be preparing for something. Things do not wear a more cheering aspect. Nothing more heard of reinforcements for us. We got a few things washed to-day for the first time; the dhobey could not iron them, and though we gave him the soap he charged enormously. We can wash as well for ourselves, but we have nearly exhausted our soap, so what we shall do I know not. A lady (Mrs. Dorin) was killed to-day while sitting in her room in Mr. Gubbins's house, by a bullet through her head. Poor thing!

she had escaped from Sutapara, having seen her husband killed before her eyes. A party of the 32nd and some Sikhs went into a house near this, where they suspected the enemy were mining this evening, but they found nothing to confirm their fears. However, they set fire to the house. We lost only one man (32nd), and he unfortunately was shot in mistake by our own people.

Thursday, July 23rd.

VERY good news, if true, this morning. A pensioner who went away before the siege began has returned with the news that a Queen's regiment, 500 Sikhs, and twelve guns were on their way here, and would be at Nawab Gunge to-day; that they had had two engagements with the enemy, in which they had beaten them well, and taken some of their guns.   The Nana of Cawnpore has also been beaten by them, and that place as well as Bithoor is in our possession.   Such is the information, — but the truth of it remains to be proved.   The force coming to our relief is, according to this account, a very small one; but I trust and pray that the Almighty will make it sufficient to aid us in this our great need.   The natives say that the insurgents are leaving this in numbers.   At any rate they have been very quiet to-day.   Part of a shell fell into the ground this evening *close* to where Mrs. Inglis and Mr. Baley were standing.   Carry is easier to-day, but there is no doubt as to her illness being small-pox, and, as yet, it appears to be even in a milder form than with Mrs. Inglis.

Information from Indians not all United

Friday, July 24th.

CARRY going on well. Dr. Scott is most kind, coming to see her every day, and says that she could not be doing better. No firing at all to-day. The insurgents must have gone away; at least, numbers of them. They say they are certainly mining. The rain was very heavy indeed last night, and Colonel Inglis was woke up by the intelligence that 400 of the enemy were inside our intrenchments. This was of course a false report, or I do not suppose that I should be sitting here to write it at this moment. Nothing more heard to-day of our reinforcements. After dark this evening Colonel Inglis had an examination of the Redan Battery, where it was believed the enemy were mining. It is not the case, fortunately.

Saturday, July 25th.

A VERY quiet day. Carry going on well. This morning, just after we were dressed, Mr. Need (a man who with his wife and two children had come here from Surora, and who live under a gateway close to us) was shot through the lungs while he was picking up a few sticks for fire-wood; he was taken to the hospital and is still alive. He had been over at our cook room about five minutes before. Dr. Scott told us a shell had hit one of the men of the 32nd on the wrist, and the poor man had been obliged to have his arm amputated. The balls are falling about and shells bursting in every direction.

Sunday, July 26th.

LAST night between twelve and one Mr. Cooper came to the door of our room and asked Mrs. Inglis if she were awake: on her replying in the affirmative, he told us that a messenger had just arrived with a letter from Colonel Tytler, the Quarter-master-General of the troops coming up to our relief, in which he said that two-thirds of the force had crossed the river between this place and Cawnpore; that they had beaten the Nana; and his army had dispersed no one knew where; that Bithoor is in our possession; that they considered their force quite equal to beating any number of the enemy they might encounter, and hoped to be here in about five or six days. This is

very cheering intelligence, and the events
of the next few days will be very momentous
to all. I fear the relief party will have to
fight their way up, and will find much difficulty in getting in here. We know the
enemy have sent out a force to meet them,
and that there must be a desperate struggle
before they reach the Residency. The
messenger went out again this evening, and
took with him a plan of the city, and directions as to the best road for coming in;
and if he delivers all safely, he is to get
5000 rupees (500l.)!! They say that there
are two Queen's regiments amongst the
troops coming. Colonel Inglis says he shall
be well satisfied if they arrive here on
Sunday next.

Mr. Lewin, of the Artillery, has been
killed to-day. Carry going on well, but
of course feels uncomfortable. There was
a short evening service in one of the mess-

rooms, to which Mrs. Inglis went. The insurgents have been very quiet to-day, and we always suspect something is going on when that is the case. It is now known beyond a doubt that they are mining, but so are we, and I hope that we shall get in and blow them up.

Monday, July 27th.

LAST night, about nine o'clock, while we were reading prayers, all undressed and ready for bed, we were suddenly stopped by heavy firing of musketry and cannon. It was preceded by a great shout, which we knew came from the enemy. At first we really thought for a moment they had got in. Mrs. Inglis knelt down and said a prayer, and our confidence was strengthened in that Almighty Power which in all our dangers is

watching over us.   The firing did not continue very long, and then succeeded a complete and deathlike silence, which was even
more painful.   It was frightful to hear the
shells whizzing over our heads.   Mrs. Inglis
remained at the door for some time to see
if any one might pass from whom she could
hear what was really going on.   I lay down
and nearly fell asleep.   A few minutes afterwards Colonel Inglis came and told us that
all was quiet, and that we might go to bed.
So we finished reading our prayers and did
so.   The night was afterwards quite quiet.
When Colonel Inglis came to see us early
this morning, he told us that Captain Shepherd had been killed last night, and, sad to
say, by our own people.   He had gone too
far out, it appears, and in the darkness of the
night was fired at by mistake.   We are all
very sorry to hear this, for he was universally
liked, and will be a great loss.   How sad

and depressing all this is, day after day!
Mrs. Need came before we were up this
morning and told us that her husband had
died in the night; and I have just heard
that one of her children has got the cholera.
Nobody could imagine all these horrors unless they witnessed them.   Nothing we wash
will dry, so our things are all damp, which
is very distressing for the children.   Colonel
Inglis told us this morning at breakfast, that
one of the enemy's mines had fallen in.
They seem to think the attack last night
was only a ruse to divert our attention from
the mining.   Mrs. Inglis went this evening
to see Mrs. Cooper, and there she heard that
the enemy are mining just under the mess-
room, close to where all the ladies are.   It
was first found out, I believe, by one of the
ladies, who heard the noise when she was in
her bath room, and called her husband to
listen to the sound.   But we are making

a counter-mine there; so I hope we may
get the best of it. The ladies are sadly
frightened, and no wonder. Nothing can
be more dreadful than the idea of mines.
The weather is very damp to-day, and at
times chilly. Carry going on well, but very
sleepy.

Tuesday, July 28th.

A QUIET night. Colonel Inglis looked
into our room between twelve and one, as
he was going his rounds, and told us that all
was right. No news this morning. One of
our servants said that guns had been heard
on the Cawnpore road by some of them,
but I think it must have been a mistake,
as no one else seems to have heard it. The
mining seems to be the engrossing topic to-
day. At twelve o'clock Mrs. Need came

and told us that her boy who had the cholera is much better; she also told us that every one was under arms just then, and that they were expecting an immediate attack, and as we heard some heavy guns we thought it likely to be the case. Tuesday and Friday are the sepoys' great fighting days. I am sure they will make some desperate struggle to get in before the reinforcements arrive. What a state to live in, never to know what these wretches are going to do! When our people were mining yesterday, they came close upon the enemy's mine, which they say was beautifully constructed, and a wax candle burning in it. They ran away as soon as they found we were near them; and in the evening we went in and blew the whole up, and completely destroyed it. As we heard the officers and men go by, they all seemed very much pleased with this affair.

In the evening Mrs. Inglis went to see Mrs. Cooper, and found Mrs. Martin sitting with her. They all had a consultation as to what they would consider best to be done in case the enemy were to get in, and whether it would be right to put an end to ourselves, if they did so, to save ourselves from the horrors we should have to endure. Some of the ladies keep laudanum and prussic acid always near them. I can scarcely think it right to have recourse to such means; it appears to me that all we have to do is, to endeavour, as far as we can, to be prepared for our death, and leave the rest in the hands of Him who knows what is best for us.

CHAP. VII.

Wednesday, July 29th.

THERE was a good deal of firing in the night, but it did not last long. I slept through it all. Why they make these attacks it is impossible to imagine. It must be to divert attention from something else. What an anxious time it is! We feel so very fearful about the reinforcements. We hear 6000 of the insurgents with 12 (some say 16) guns have gone out to meet them. I fear that they will have much difficulty in getting in. These mines are dreadful, and Colonel Inglis tells us that the enemy have regular Sappers. In fact, I think no one supposed they would have been capable of doing

all that they have done.   Another message
was sent to the relieving force yesterday,
with a duplicate of the plan of our position
here, in case the first should not reach its
destination.

Thursday, July 30th.

YESTERDAY, about six o'clock, while we
were at dinner, the greatest excitement prevailed, the sound of distant guns being heard,
and loud cheering from English voices.
Every one was rushing about in a frantic
manner, exclaiming that the relief had arrived; and one would have supposed that
they were actually at the gates, waiting for
admittance.   We all, like the rest, rushed
out to see what it was, and went over to
Carry, who, we thought, might be frightened;
but she was quietly sitting up in her bed

All the servants were calling out that the regiments had arrived, and the ayah began to say her prayers. Colonel Palmer rushed up to Mrs. Inglis, shook hands with her, and congratulated her on the arrival of the reinforcements. For my own self, I must say I had no sooner got out of the room where we dined, than I began to think it was just as likely to be the enemy getting in. The excitement was tremendous, but lasted only for a few minutes, and then it subsided. Nobody knew what was the matter. The only thing that was quite evident was, that the relief had *not* arrived, and it was impossible to imagine what the guns in the distance, which sounded more like a salute than any thing else, could be for. Some said that yesterday was the day on which the insurgents intended to proclaim a king, others supposed that a victory might have been gained by them. Colonel Inglis made us all go to dinner

again, and was very angry that there should
have been such a frantic demonstration without any cause for it, as he thought it
would do a great deal of harm when the
reaction took place, and would greatly shake
the confidence of our own few sepoys. It is
impossible to help feeling disappointed after
a thing of that kind, and to-day I think every
one looks more or less dispirited.

Whilst at breakfast, Captain Wilson came,
and reported to Colonel Inglis that numbers
of the enemy were to be seen in the direction of the Bridge of Boats, coming from the
Cawnpore side; palanquins with quantities
of men running alongside of them, and that
tents and other appendages to an army had
been seen with them. Colonel Inglis said
that if they went over the bridge he should
consider all was right; but if they went in
the other direction, it would look suspicious.
Captain Wilson said he did not know what to

think, and looked, I thought, rather disheartened. About twelve o'clock, Colonel Inglis came, and told us that they could see nothing more of these people, but that charpoys with wounded men in them had been plainly seen. What an anxious time it is ! How one longs to know what it all can mean ! If there has been an action fought, and our troops have been victorious, I think we *must* hear something of it this evening. On the other hand, I do think, if the insurgents had gained a victory over us, we should have heard noise and shouting in the bazaar.

Carry up to-day for the first time. Dr. Scott told us that Mr. Grant, an officer belonging to a Native Regiment, had died this morning from a wound in his hand. His wife and child also died (of fever, I believe) a few days ago, but he did not know it, poor man. Mr. Bonham, our best artillery officer, has been seized with small-pox this morn-

ing.   Poor old Colonel Halford died yesterday from complete break-up, I believe.   How
sad for his wife and daughter !   This morning
has been very fine, but we had a heavy
shower of rain about two o'clock.   It is
only wonderful that any one keeps well at
such a time.   The want of exercise and air,
and the difficulty of keeping one's clothes or
any thing else even tolerably clean, are great
trials to those who have never suffered from
such evils before, but truly they are trifles in
comparison with the great trials so many
breaking hearts have lately had to undergo.

Friday, July 31st.

CARRY sat up nearly the whole day yesterday,
and did not seem weak or even tired, and it
is quite wonderful how rapidly the marks of
her illness are disappearing.   No news what-

ever this morning; the night was quiet. Johnny still not quite right. Dr. Scott saw him this morning. This is a most lovely day; the air is quite delicious. What can have become of our reinforcements? There is a native report to-day that some bridge is broken down, and that they will have to go ten miles round. I have been washing a few things.

Saturday, August 1st.

LAST night was quiet, but this morning the enemy have been firing heavy guns, which they have brought over from the Muchee Bhawun. All the guns they had here have gone out with their force — at least so it is supposed — to meet our reinforce-- ments coming in, and as nothing can be heard of them it is imagined that the insurgents have been cutting up the roads to prevent their getting in. Heard to-day that another lady, Mrs. Clarke, died yesterday. We also heard that Mr. Ommanney was dead, and Dr. Scott said there had been some fresh cases of cholera this morning.

Sunday, August 2nd.

THIS day last week we certainly expected that the relief would have been in or heard of to-day; but nothing whatever in the shape of news from them has yet arrived, so our prospects are less and less cheering. Colonel Inglis read the morning's service, but was interrupted by heavy firing. I believe, however, that it was blank ammunition which the enemy were firing, as this day is a great festival with them, which they call the Buckra Eid, the day the Mussulmen have their sacrifices. Dr. Scott came and saw Johnny and Carry, the former much better. No small-pox; the latter he thought looking a good deal pulled down. At twelve o'clock Mr. Harris gave a short service, to which Mrs. Inglis went. Colonel Inglis returned after a short time, and finished reading the prayers to us when the firing ceased. The rest of the day was quiet. The enemy, to the number of about 300, were seen going off in the direction of Cawnpore, but they have left quite enough here to annoy us with their shells and bullets. Carry came to dinner for the first time to-day. In the evening Mrs. Inglis went to see Mrs. Cooper, and just before we went to bed we walked outside the Sikhs' compound, close to the Begum's House. The night was most lovely, and bright moonlight, and though I do not suppose we walked above twenty or, at most, thirty paces, it is nearly five weeks since I have been so far.

We heard a good deal of shouting before we went to bed, and, as usual, the enemy's bugles, to which now little attention seems to be paid.

Monday, August 3rd.

STILL nothing heard of our relief, and the days appear months while this dreadful state of things is going on. Colonel Inglis told us this morning that one man went out to our reinforcements four days ago, and that he is certain to return if he can. He has gone all the way round by Marian, and is to return by Chinhut. They seem to think he might possibly be here to-morrow.

It is now said we have only provisions for twenty days more. What is to become of us if our relief does not arrive before that time! By some negligence six fine bullocks were smothered in the bousse yesterday — a great loss at such a time.   The commissariat butcher came to ask for three of Colonel Inglis's goats this morning, to kill them for food, which looks as if we are beginning to run short of meat.   In the midst of all this, it is scarcely possible to believe, but it is nevertheless true, that we have had to-day servants coming round with lists of ladies' clothes for sale, and a box with four very smart bonnets in it was also being taken round to see if any one would purchase them.   What a strange contrast do such facts present to the awful scenes around us and the feelings that we are impressed with ! It is dreadful to think that we may be short of provisions.

Every morning before she is dressed Mrs. Inglis weighs out every thing for our daily consumption with her own hands, and so good is her management that she is always able to give a little arrowroot or sugar to a

sick child, and has two or three times succeeded in making little puddings for invalids
without an egg and with but a very limited
quantity of sugar. Mrs. Inglis paid her
usual visit to Mrs. Case, but heard no news.
We spoke to Mr. and Mrs. Martin as they
passed through our courtyard; they told us
poor little Tiny is very ill.

Tuesday, August 4th.

As usual, I begin with the same remark, No
news! Nothing heard of the relief. The
night was quiet, but I suffered so much from
violent pain in my face and head, that I hardly
slept at all. Colonel Inglis is not very well;
he has been out too much this morning
in the sun. We dined in our small room,
and just as we had finished dinner, a shell
burst in our courtyard, causing great con-

fusion amongst the inhabitants. Our punkah Coolie left the punkah, and darted into the room. He had seen it coming. It made a great noise, but fortunately hurt no one. A short time before, one fell *close* to Mrs. Cooper and her children, but fortunately did not burst for want of powder. Of course she was a good deal frightened. Dr. Scott told us this morning that poor Major Anderson is very ill.

Wednesday, August 5th.

IT is raining heavily to-day, and therefore it is lucky we did not wash, as it was our intention; there is so much difficulty in getting any thing dry. Colonel Inglis is better to-day, but looks very tired.

Yesterday our servants came and told us about four P.M., that they heard guns in the distance. Mrs. Inglis and I went out and listened, and thought we heard them also, but as no one else did, I suppose we must have been mistaken. How weary one gets, hearing nothing of our relief! These wretches around us were shouting a great deal last night, looting the city again, I suppose; and the cries we hear must be often of those in distress.

A man of the 32nd was killed in the hospital to-day. He was taking something to one of his comrades, when he was shot through the heart! I believe he is the second or third who has been thus shot in the hospital. This must be very disheartening to the sick people. I have heard that since the commencement of this siege we have already lost 180 men of the 32nd *only!!*

Thursday, August 6th.

LAST night, while we were at prayers, a shell burst close to our door, just behind the punkah wallah. It struck into the ground with a great noise, and made us all rush to the door to see where it had fallen. Not many minutes afterwards a bullet came close to the ayah, and with a tremendous clatter broke a plate, which she had beside her. This also was just at our door. Several other shots were fired into our little court-yard, and so near did they appear, that Mrs. Inglis began to think they must be taking particular aim at this place, thinking that Colonel Inglis slept here. I believe that there was some heavy firing during the night, but I am thankful to say I slept well, and did not hear it.

This morning poor Mr. Studdy, of the 32nd, has had one of his arms taken off by a round shot in the Residency. I hear that he is likely to lose both, and that it is even doubtful if he will live. Poor young man! We were very sorry indeed to hear of this, he has behaved so well all through the siege. No news of any kind. It is now twelve days since we have heard any thing from outside, and our relief was then supposed to be within three marches of us. To-morrow we and the servants are to be put on half rations. How dreadful it will be when they are obliged to commence that with the fighting men !

Yesterday evening Mrs. Inglis and I walked through the Sikhs' compound and Begum Khotee. When one sees the walls and narrow roads within which we are enclosed, *escape* seems an impossibility if these wretches

were to get in! I would give much to know
what has become of my poor ayah; she would
be a treasure to us here.   A very warm, but
fine day.

CHAP. VIII.

Friday, August 7th.

LAST night about eleven o'clock, just before we went to bed (for we were later than usual), Colonel Inglis told us that two messengers had just arrived, bringing news of the reinforcements. One of the men had been sent out about ten days ago with a letter to the officer commanding the relief. It appeared that he had been in our neighbourhood four days without being able to get in. He brought a letter with him, which, unfortunately, he lost just before he arrived. He states that there are four European regiments, besides artillery, sappers and miners, and Sikhs. They are only able to march about

three miles a day, as they intrench their camp
every night, and the enemy have done all
they can to break up the roads and impede
their progress. He says that there have been
two actions fought, and both times our
troops were victorious. One man says we
have taken twenty-three, the other eighteen,
guns from the enemy. He says a retrograde
movement had been made by our troops; the
reason is supposed to be that the Nana was
collecting a force in their rear, and they had
gone back to attack them. From the account
of their position and distance from us, it is
possible they might be here in two or three
days; but Colonel Inglis says he shall feel
very thankful if they arrive in eight. The
man says that in the city here the insurgents
talk of blowing us up by mining, or starving
us out.

This morning, two sergeants of the 32nd
(both good and useful men) have been mor-

tally wounded. A shell burst, and they rushed out to see where it had fallen, when another burst at the spot where they were, and wounded them both dreadfully in their right arms. Dr. Scott says, Mr. Studdy is going on well. His arm (the right one) was amputated, but he was able to bear it, and they do not think now, as was at first supposed, that he had received a severe inward bruise. They gave him a bottle of champagne before the operation, as he was too weak for chloroform, and he bore it, poor fellow, without saying a word.

Mr. Thornhill and Captain Hardinge came in while we were at dinner. A report had just before been made to Colonel Inglis, that a body of men were seen gathering in the direction of Mr. Innes' house, and they came to say that it was a false alarm. After dinner Mrs. Inglis read us the deposition of the messenger who came in last night ; and certainly there is a great stamp of truth about it; especially from one or two quite native and original statements which he makes. One was, that when the enemy fled, they left behind them thousands of *shoes !* It puzzles us all very much to imagine how our messengers carry the letters about with them, small as they are, for they wear so little clothing, that it must be most difficult to secrete them; one was brought in a quill, and another, I believe, in a shaving brush; the man passing for a barber among the insurgents.

Saturday, August 8th.

EVERY thing going on as usual. A very warm day; not much firing going on. The servants have begun to-day to grind their own food, a process which Mrs. Inglis says they do not like at all. We have just seen a letter which is about to be sent out to the relieving force, and certainly it was a curiosity. The whole thing was not larger than this ☐; indeed, I do not think it was quite so long. It was a piece of a quill sealed at each end, the letter rolled up inside. One could scarcely have imagined it possible that it could have been made up into such a tiny thing, but yet the letter contained 253 words, and some of them very long. I should like to know where the man will carry it; he might put it in his ear. I am very glad I saw it, as otherwise I could not have had an idea that it *could* be made so small. A private of the 32nd was killed at Mr. Gubbins's to-day, and a poor ayah was badly wounded.

Sunday, August 9th.

POOR Mr. Studdy died this morning. The severe inward contusion which he received appears to have been the chief cause of his death. He is much regretted; a very promising young officer, and had behaved so very well during all the siege! One of the sergeants who were wounded on Friday, died this morning also. Divine service in the mess-room at twelve : Mrs. Inglis went. A quiet day.

Monday, August 10th.

WHEN we went to breakfast this morning, we saw a Sikh sitting in the room, who had come in last night; I believe he had not been beyond the city, but his deposition has not yet been taken. About twelve P.M., as I was sitting at the table writing, Carry washing our things, and Mrs. Inglis working, we were suddenly alarmed by what appeared to us a great shaking of the earth, followed by a *dreadful* noise, such as I never wish to hear again. It was indescribable, and sounded as if the whole earth was coming against us; it was a mine exploding without doing any harm. We thought it had been in the ladies' room, especially when we saw Mrs. Cooper, her nurse and children, and Mrs. Radclyffe with hers, all coming over to our room as fast as they could. Poor Mrs. C. was dreadfully frightened. We laid her on one of our couches, and gave her some wine. A fierce attack followed the explosion of the mine, and a round shot fell close to our door; half a yard nearer, and it must have been into the room. It sounded altogether very frightful, as these attacks always do. In about twenty minutes Colonel Inglis came and told us that we had better all go into the large room, as we were safer there from the round shot, so there we all adjourned, each of us seizing hold of a child. I got hold of little Charley. For about an hour and a half the firing was loud and frequent. When the mine exploded our servants all rushed into our room, and for a moment appeared alarmed; but it is quite wonderful to see them sitting outside while the firing is going on, washing their clothes and pursuing their occupations as usual, just as if nothing was going on.

Colonel Inglis had a wonderful escape; one of the orderly-room clerks of the 32nd was shot down and mortally wounded as he was standing between him and Colonel

Palmer; I believe the man actually fell
against him. Poor Sergeant Campbell (32nd)
was killed to-day, a most excellent man. I
used to see him very often when we were
coming down from Peshawur, and always
heard him spoken of as being a very good
and superior man. Mrs. Ouseley had a
little boy this morning, and Mrs. Barwell
yesterday. *giving birth under siege*

Tuesday, August 11th.

LAST night about nine o'clock, just as we were
preparing for bed, there was another attack.
We were sitting outside our door, as usual,
when we observed what a complete lull there
was, and how wonderfully quiet every thing
appeared to be. We had hardly said the
words, when a tremendous fire of musketry
and round shot began. The noise was fear-

ful ; the attack lasted about an hour, and during that time the firing was the sharpest and loudest we have yet had. We did not undress till it was over, when Colonel Inglis came and told us that all was quiet, and not one of our men had been hit. There was an attack while we were at dinner, which they say was the most fierce of all, though it did not sound so to us. The enemy made a tremendous rush, and got so near that they seized hold of some of our men's firelocks. They seemed determined to get in, but I am sure they will not do so without a most desperate struggle. I cannot help thinking that they must have heard something about the relief being near, and that is the reason why they are making such desperate attempts. I hear that they say that in less than a week they will have murdered all the "Sahib logues." Captain Hardinge told Mrs. Inglis last night, that just before the attack was commenced yes-

terday morning, two guns were distinctly
heard in the distance by two or three people.
What they were we have not yet heard.
Three of our men have had a most wonderful escape. They were blown up by the
mine, and actually thrown among the insurgents in the midst of the heavy firing, but got
back again quite safely, — one of them being
only a little singed.

A dreadful accident has happened this
morning. Part of the Residency has fallen
in, and five or six men of the 32nd have
been buried in the ruins. When Colonel
Inglis was there a short time ago, two of the
poor men had been extricated as far as their
heads only, and could just speak, with the
help of brandy being poured down their
throats. Their sufferings must be dreadful; and they, as well as those who are
digging them out, are under fire the whole
time. It certainly is the most dreadful

thing that has happened to us since the siege began; and now when the life of every man is of such value, one cannot sufficiently lament such a loss. Poor Major Anderson is dying. It is just reported that guns have been heard towards cantonments.

Wednesday, August 12th.

A GOOD deal of firing went on during the night. The enemy were as usual making an attack somewhere. The nights are dreadful; one looks forward so anxiously for the first ray of daylight. Then the day arrives with no news of our relief. One's heart sickens at all this delay, and knowing nothing of what is going on outside these gates.

They say that we might, with very great

difficulty and pinching, as far as provisions go, hold out one month longer, but after that there will not be a hope for us; and now the natives have a report that the reinforcements will not be here for two months. If such should be the case, what a fate is before us! May God, in his infinite mercy, grant that we may be prepared, through the merits of our Saviour, for whatever is to happen to us! An attack is going on while I am writing, and I cannot help thinking what would be the feelings of any lady suddenly transported from quiet, peaceful England to this room, around which the bullets are whizzing, the round shot falling, and now and then a loud explosion, as if a mine were blowing up, which I think is almost worse than all the sharp and fast fire of the musketry. It is an awful time; and words could never make any one understand all that we have undergone during now nearly three months (ever since the 17th of May). Poor Major Anderson is dead. He was a great favourite, and is universally regretted. The attack yesterday, I believe, hastened his end. His death has made poor Dr. Scott very ill again. His head has become quite affected. Some of our people went out to-day to blow up a house near this, but unfortunately failed in the attempt, as the enemy were prepared for them, and this was the cause of all the firing we heard. I am thankful to say that we had not a man of ours killed or wounded, which to us appears almost incredible, after such a heavy fire. Little Ada Radclyffe died this morning; she had been ailing for some time, and at last it turned to cholera. An ayah also died of cholera close to this yesterday. We had a few potatoes for dinner yesterday, a thing we had not seen for more than a month. They were found in one of the rooms. Mrs. Inglis is not looking well; the want of air, exercise, and proper nourishment begins to tell more or less on every one.

Thursday, August 13th.

A VERY hot day. After breakfast our people blew up the house which they attempted yesterday. The explosion made very little noise, which surprised us, as we expected it would be very loud. There was very little firing on the part of the enemy; but this is a fast day with them, so, perhaps, not a fighting one. Mrs. Cooper's nurse, with the two children, came over to our room when they expected the explosion. She told us that little Tiny Martin died this morning, also a little child which Mrs. Pitt had the care of. I heard this morning that Captain Power died four or five days ago.

Friday, August 14th.

I FELT very unwell yesterday, and went to bed early, but was awoke soon after by heavy firing. It lasted but a short time, and the night afterwards was quiet. We are still without news of any kind, and the enemy are painfully still this morning. They must be plotting mischief. A great many children are suffering dreadfully from want of proper nourishment; it is so very difficult to procure milk.

Yesterday afternoon a very respectable-looking person, with a little baby in her arms, came to the door of our room, and after asking Mrs. Inglis if she was " the brigadier's lady," said she had come to beg a little milk for her child, as she was afraid she should lose it if she could not get proper nourish-

ment for it. Her simple story, told in such
a genuine honest manner, affected us all,
though one hears sad things every day. She
said that her little baby was born the first day
of the attack ; her husband (whose name was
Beale, an overseer of the works) was shot
through the lungs, and died almost immediately. From grief and fretting she had
lost all her milk, and had nothing to give the
poor little thing. She told us that she had
lost three children — one she described as
being a beautiful child, and was very anxious
if she could to rear this one, to take it to her
friends in England. Mrs. Inglis asked her
where her home was ; she said, in Kent, and
that her father is a clergyman there, and her
husband's father was an officer in the army.
She said she had every thing she wanted but
nourishment for her child, and though many
in this place are doubtless in the same sad
plight, her plain tale, told without the

slightest appearance of wishing to excite pity, made an impression on me I shall not easily forget. Dr. Scott paid us a long visit this morning; he was quite out of spirits. We are all very anxious he should come and live in our large room, as we think it would be more cheerful for him.

Saturday, August 15th.

YESTERDAY a metah belonging to a native doctor of the 7th Cavalry came in. He had been shut out on the first day of the siege, and therefore had been in the way of hearing something of what is going on outside. His deposition agreed with other native reports which we had heard. He said our reinforcements are still at Mhow, waiting for the China force to join them; but that 900 (we suppose an advance-guard) had come on to a place much nearer, and had an engagement with the enemy the day before yesterday, and captured two guns from them. He describes the sepoys round this place as getting disheartened, but still in great numbers. Dr. Scott came over this morning, and took up his abode in the large room in our court-yard. We think it will do him good being with us all. The rain was very heavy last night, and the lightning vivid.

CHAP. IX.

Sunday, August 16th.

LAST night the pensioner who went out to Colonel Tytler with Colonel Inglis's letter of the 8th instant returned. He brought with him a few lines from Colonel Tytler to Mr. Gubbins, dated 4th August, saying that the reinforcements were on their way to Lucknow, and expected to be with us in three or four days; but the deposition of the messenger stated they had had another engagement with the enemy and had returned to Cawnpore, so when they will be here is as much a matter of conjecture as ever.

I hear that the longest time we can now

hold out, as regards provisions, is to the 10th of next month. The messenger states that he delivered Colonel Inglis's letter and plans to Colonel Tytler. He describes the insurgents as being very numerous, and says that they have proclaimed some child "king." There is a story that the messenger was asked by some of the people with the relieving force, "*If the Sahib logues here were able to take rides every evening and morning!*" If that is true, they have not the slightest idea of our position, which is dreadful to think of, but we must keep up *hope*.

Monday, August 17th.

EVERY thing is still very quiet, indeed far too much so, for the insurgents must be plotting mischief when they are not busy with an attack. Azaib and Din Mahomed

went to the Residency to-day, to see where
our few remaining boxes are. They gave a
miserable account of them. A round shot
has been through one of them, and, of course,
every thing inside was broken. They are
all used for barricades, and some are in
water. I would give any thing to have one
of them, which contains some precious letters
and some of our favourite things, nearly all
presents. I fear there are but few of them
we shall ever see again. Mr. and Mrs.
Thornhill and Mrs. Barber came and sat
out here in the evening. Mr. T. was looking very ill, having had fever and been
hit by a spent bullet a few days ago.

Tuesday, August 18*th.*

THIS morning about six o'clock we were all
roused by the explosion of one of the enemy's mines. Six drummers were buried in
it; three have been got out, the other three
still remain. It is to be hoped that the
poor fellows are dead; for they say it is
impossible to extricate them, as the place is
so completely under the enemy's fire. Two
officers had a wonderful escape: one was
in bed at the time, but they were both
blown up in the air and came down again
without being hurt. The enemy have certainly gained an advantage to-day. It is
only wonderful that they do not get in
altogether, so numerous as they are; but
they advance by two and three at a time.
It appears that their leader came on quite

close this morning waving his sword and beckoning on his men, but he was shot dead at once, as well as the few others who came after him. 3 P.M.—Just heard that *we* have retaken the position which the enemy got possession of this morning, and we have not lost a man.

Wednesday, August 19th.

YESTERDAY was a most successful day for us; for not only was the position which the enemy had taken in the morning re-taken by us in the afternoon, but Johannes' house was blown up, and our people got out farther than they have hitherto been, and some fresh mines were discovered. I should like to be able to give an account of the proceedings of the day, but do not sufficiently understand the different positions of the place to do so. Colonel Inglis was much pleased with his day's work, but was dreadfully knocked up in the evening, and did not return to dinner till past seven. We all thought we should have a very quiet night, but at nine o'clock, just as we were going to bed, the enemy commenced an attack. It lasted only a short time, but the firing for the time was very loud. Mrs. Pierce was so frightened that she came over here with her little child and remained till it was over. A man of the 32nd was killed yesterday. There is an old woman, a resident of Lucknow, living now in this compound, who is most anxious to go out as a spy, and says that she will undertake to take a letter to the reinforcements, or even to go to Calcutta if it were necessary; but to judge by the way she walks about here, she would be a long time getting there. She says that she could disguise herself so as to be able to pass out among the insurgents. A round shot fell in our court-yard to-day, close to the head of one of the goats, but fortunately did not hurt any one.

Thursday, August 20th.

COLONEL Inglis was very much knocked up yesterday; indeed, I do not think he can stand all this wear and tear much longer. It rained heavily last night, and we could not sit out as usual. Dr. Scott had his tea with us in our room. We all fancied last night had been very quiet, but Colonel Inglis says that there was a great deal of shouting and noise of tomtom, and that he had a disturbed night. A good deal of shelling has been going on this morning, but it is mostly our own. . Captain Lowe and Mr.

Browne came in while we were at dinner. It rained in the evening a good deal. A poor little child next door to us died of cholera; it was only taken ill about one o'clock and it was dead before seven. The poor mother was in a dreadful state just before it died, and afterwards perfectly calm. While we were undressing she came and asked if we had an empty box we could give her to bury the poor little thing in. We had not one long enough.

Friday, August 21st.

JUST after we were in bed there was a great deal of firing, but it lasted a short time. There was a second attack during the night, I am thankful to say, however, that I did not hear it. I was awoke (it was scarcely daylight, and our lamp still burning) by Mrs. Pierce, with her little child in her arms, standing at the foot of my bed ; she said she had spoken, but we were all asleep and none had answered her. She appeared very much frightened, and awaking in that confused way, I really at first imagined the insurgents had got in. I tried to awaken Mrs. Inglis, but she was so sound asleep that I could not make her hear. Mrs. Pierce then told me that our people were going to blow up Johannes' house, that the explosion would be very loud indeed, and that 100 men and Colonel Inglis and several officers had just passed by on their way towards the ladies' square. I succeeded at last in awakening Mrs. Inglis, and soon after the mine exploded. It shook our room, but the noise was not loud. When it was over Mrs. Pierce went away, but she appeared very much frightened. We soon heard that the whole thing had been very successful. We had one man killed, one mortally wounded, two severely, and two slightly. It was sad to see the poor creatures carried through our court-yard before we were up. Another child of the poor Dedmans was seized with cholera this morning, and is not expected to live. Captain Barlow died this morning, he had been ill for some days. Captain Lowe was slightly wounded to-day; he had a very narrow escape of his life. A shell burst close to the bed on which he was lying, and took off the arm of a man beside him. Mr. Edmonstone came and paid us a visit yesterday evening. He is looking much better. This has been a very quiet day, scarcely any firing at all. While we were at dinner Captain Wilson brought in a boy about eleven years old who had come over from the insurgents. He had been picking up bullets, and came

near our sentry, who laid hold of him
and got him in. He said that the enemy
had been stealing some arms belonging to us
at the Redan. It really is a perfect wonder
to me that they do not get in altogether.
He did not appear to give any particular information, but he describes the enemy as
being in great numbers, and says that they
intend going out and fighting our reinforcements in the open field when they arrive.
Carry not at all well yesterday, but better
to-day.

Saturday, August 22nd.

LAST night was very quiet. Yesterday a
sergeant of the 84th was killed — a very good
man. From what he said before his death it
would appear that he was well connected, and

had a relative in this garrison. He had enlisted under the name of Allen. Dr. Scott left us to-day, as he considered it necessary to be at the hospital, Dr. Boyd having been taken ill. In the evening we walked up to the end of the road past the Ommanneys' house, farther than we have ever been since we were shut up here, and yet it is but a few paces. We lost three men yesterday.

Sunday, August 23rd.

THERE was Divine Service and the Holy Communion in the mess-room this morning. It was a melancholy Sunday indeed; three more men killed! While we were at dinner Mr. Foster came to say that the back verandah of the Residency had fallen in : fortunately no one was hurt. Dr. Scott came and had a cup of tea with us in the evening. He told us that distant guns had been heard from different places, but one gets weary of hearing reports which never come to any thing. The Dedman's child is better, its illness is not cholera.

Monday, August 24th.

A MAN came from outside this morning and brought intelligence that our reinforcements are still at Cawnpore, the China force not having yet joined them, so that in fact they were nearer to us this day last month. Our people here seem to think that the man is a spy, and no great reliance is placed on what he says. He represents the insurgents as having suffered a good deal, and says that ninety were killed in the explosion of the mine the other day. The man was once a kitmaghar of Mrs. Hayes, and lived after-wards with the Coopers. So many children are sick now that one hears nearly every day of some one dying, and many children and grown up persons too are suffering from boils and eruptions on the skin.

Tuesday, August 25th.

ANOTHER sergeant of the 84th was mor-tally wounded yesterday, and one of the 32nd died of cholera. Mr. M'Crea, an officer of the engineers, was also wounded in the arm yesterday. Last night at twelve o'clock we were awoke by tremendous firing. The enemy made a sharp attack, but it only lasted a short time, and all the harm they did was slightly wounding two men of the 13th. To us, lying quietly in our beds watching the flashing of the guns and listening to the loud report of the cannon and bursting of the shells, it seems almost impossible to think otherwise than that they are rushing in upon us.

To-day a suspicion seems to be afloat as to the fidelity of our Sikhs, but merely, I believe, because they were overheard saying they wanted their pay. Dr. Scott came to see us, but would not remain for tea.

Wednesday, August 26th.

WHEN the ayah came in last night, she arrived with a very melancholy face, and told us that the insurgents had been knocking a hole in some place near the ladies' rooms, and having already made a good road to it, they were sure to get in there in three or four days. She also said she had heard that our

I

reinforcements would not be here for three or four months. I wonder that we are not all getting more disheartened than we appear to be. I did not sleep well last night, and really to hear the firing going on the whole night long whenever one happens to awake is most wearing.

Nothing new this morning. Dr. Scott came to pay us his usual evening's visit. We thought him looking ill. He told us that Mr. Webb of the 32nd had just been killed. About eight P.M. Captain Wilson with a native came to Colonel Inglis's room. We at once imagined that a letter had been received from the relieving force, and remained in anxious suspense for some time, but we soon found that hewasonly a spy from *inside*, who had come to report on the feeling which pervades our native troops in the garrison.

Thursday, August 27th.

COLONEL INGLIS had a most merciful escape last night.   He was standing on the bastion at Mr. Gubbins's house, close to Mr. Webb when he was killed.   They saw the round shot coming, and went down to avoid it, but it hit Mr. Webb, and a native who was with him, killing them both instantaneously.   It makes one shudder to think how death is hovering about and around us all; busy indeed has he been amongst this little garrison.

Mrs. Thornhill had a little girl last night. Sir Henry Lawrence's things are being sold to-day; heard of a ham being sold for 7*l.*, and a tin of soup sufficient only for one day's dinner for 1*l.* 5*s.* ! ! !   Money has ceased to be of any value, and people are giving un-heard-of prices for stores of any kind — one dozen brandy, 20*l.* ; one small box of ver-micelli, 5*l.* ; four small cakes of chocolate, 2*l.* 10*s.* ! ! !

At Mr. Gubbins's house, to-day, one man was killed, and another mortally wounded, both 32nd men. This evening has been very hot, and we could not sit out at all. The day has been very quiet.

Friday, August 28th.

A QUIET night. Our people appear to think there will be another attack on the 31st, or perhaps sooner. They have been taking down the large doors in the room where we dine, to form barricades. A man of the 32nd killed to-day. We have not heard much firing.   A lovely moonlight night. Mrs. Inglis and I walked up and down the little space we have for nearly an hour; our topic—the only one from which we derive support at present and hope for the future— religion.

Saturday, August 29th.

A MESSENGER came in last night from Cawnpore, bringing a letter from General Havelock to Colonel Inglis, as follows:—

"Cawnpore, August 24, 1857.

" MY DEAR COLONEL,

    " I have your letter of the 16th inst. I can only say, Hold on, and do not negotiate, but rather perish sword in hand. Sir Colin

Campbell, who came out at a day's notice to command, upon the news arriving of General Anson's death, promises me fresh troops, and you will be my first care. The reinforcements may reach me in from twenty to twenty-five days, and I will prepare every thing for a march on Lucknow.

"Yours very sincerely,

"H. HAVELOCK,

"Major-General.

"Colonel Inglis, H.M. 32nd Regiment."

I fear that this will sadly dishearten all the natives inside, and with the weak state of our garrison, how are we to hold out a month longer? Faith and confidence in our Heavenly Father's protecting care will, I trust, support us under all the trials and difficulties which are before us. The messenger states, in his deposition, that there are three

Indian regiments at Cawnpore; that the fall
of Delhi was expected in twenty days; that
we have a very large force surrounding it.
The insurgents had ceased to fire on Agra.
The Nana at Cawnpore had been beaten twice
by our troops, but fifty Europeans had been
killed by falling into an ambush of (I think)
the 42nd Native Infantry. He says that the
insurgents are very numerous about us
(11,000); that they have a council of war
every day, and every day order an attack, but
to-morrow and Tuesday are the great days
they talk of. He says the rebels *say* the Sikhs
and men of the 48th and 71st Native Infantry in here are in league with them, and
will desert us, but *he* does not believe it.
He says that they hear from people who go in
and out every thing that goes on inside, and he
represents Lucknow as being a most difficult
place to get to, or have any communication
with. The worst of all this is, that if the siege

continues as long as we should of course suppose it will, what a loss of valuable life there must be before it is raised!

A mine has been blown up by our people most successfully this morning, close to the ladies' room. They needed something to put them all in good spirits to-day. This morning has been very wet. Mrs. Bankes moved from Mr. Gubbins's house to some room near Mrs. Cooper's. She gave Mrs. Inglis a dreadful account of the number of round shot which went into the upper story of Mr. Gubbins's house. One came in while Mr. and Mrs. Gubbins were in bed; it struck the foot of the bed, and made them jump up a good deal frightened. Another poor soldier of the 32nd was killed last night.

Sunday, August 30th.

HEARD this morning that twelve of our people from inside had deserted, — three drummers and their wives, a kitmaghar of Mrs. Cooper's, and other servants. The Gubbins's confidential servant, taking 400 rupees with him, and some others belonging to the same establishment, went off a few days ago. The Martins' youngest child died on Saturday. This day has been very quiet, and no attack as was anticipated.

Monday, August 31st.

MRS. INGLIS is not feeling well to-day, and does not look at all herself. This want of air and exercise, and prison life, tells more or less on all of us. Very hot. One of the 32nd men killed at the Gubbins's.

Tuesday, September 1st.

LAST night about nine o'clock some heavy firing commenced, and we of course imagined it to be the signal for an attack, so carried off the three children into the large room, but did not remain there more than half an hour, as it turned out to be nothing. Colonel Inglis came in for a moment, and said that he did not think it would be much. I am always sorry when he gets so disturbed at night. He has not slept with his clothes off since the 16th of May! To-day up to four o'clock very quiet. It is now stated that upwards of 300 *Europeans* have been killed since the commencement of the siege.

Wednesday, September 2nd.

YESTERDAY passed off very quietly, but two men of the Artillery were killed at the post-office in the evening, and a very serious loss they are, our trained men of this arm being so few.   There was a good deal of musketry between ten and twelve last night.   We had all our boxes and furniture moved out of our room this morning ; carpets taken up, and all cleaned ; day very hot.   When Mrs. Inglis went to see Mrs. Cooper this evening, she heard that five babies had been buried during the night.

Thursday, September 3rd.

A SAD thing has happened.   Mr. Birch, an engineer officer, was killed by mistake by one of our own sentries last night.   He was out on the fortification reconnoitring the enemy's ground, and the sentry, not having been warned, fired and shot him. He lived three or four hours, and was quite sensible to the last. He has left a wife, sister, and brother, all dependent on him. Poor Vokins died yesterday. We managed to get four tablecloths washed, but they do not look much better than they did before they went. Carry is washing our clothes to-day. Very hot. Got two of our boxes from the Residency, but there is not much in them that is of use to us now. Nearly every thing we have is, I fear, lost in the Serah Roti. I have just been grieving over Carry's nice dressing box, besides a variety of other things endeared to us by fond associations, which I never expect to see again.

Saw Dr. Brydon out this evening for the first time since he was wounded; also saw Dr. Boyd, who is quite well again. Day quiet.

Friday, September 4th.

QUIET last night; but one man (32nd) mortally wounded. Nothing going on this morning, except a native report that our force was to cross the river to-day. If we could only hear for a certainty that they had actually started for Lucknow it would cheer us up a little; and, indeed, we need it. There is a native report that Maun Sing is here with 6,000 men. A man of the 32nd killed to-day. Major Bruce also killed while we were at dinner. He has left a wife and large family. The native soldiers of his regiment would not allow any one but themselves to touch him after he was dead, and carried him to the grave, which is a great mark of their affection, as it is against their caste to touch a Christian after he is dead.

Saturday, September 5th.

Mrs. Inglis was called up at three this morning to Mrs. Cooper, who was taken ill: and she was brought over to our large room. She had a little girl about five o'clock, and is doing very well. About ten A.M. the enemy blew up two mines. The first was the most severe shock we have felt, but I am thankful to say they did no harm. An attack succeeded in which it appears the insurgents got well punished, though they had been preparing for it some time, and to-day I hear brought up their cavalry. I have not heard of any one being wounded, except one poor boy of the

32nd, who has lost his hand. I believe the enemy were more determined in their attack to-day than they have ever shown themselves before. A great part of the wall in the ladies' room was knocked down by a round shot yesterday while we were at dinner. A pensioner and a sepoy were killed to-day.

We have now to dine and breakfast in our little room. The only change we had in the twenty-four hours was going into the other room for our meals; so we are greater prisoners than ever. The cooing of some doves belonging to the servants, and a green tree before our door, are the only pleasant things that we have in our captivity!

Sunday, September 6th.

WHILE Colonel Inglis was reading the morning service there was a good deal of firing, but the rest of the day has been quiet. An artilleryman killed. Weather very hot now. Dr. Scott came to see us yesterday evening ; he looked ill. A native report says that the king is to leave this place to-morrow.

Monday, September 7th.

AT ten last night, what appeared to us a fierce attack in the direction of the Brigade Mess commenced, and the firing was so loud that, each of us taking up a child, went over to Mrs. Cooper's room. Never saw such a small child as hers in my life. We did not stay there long, as the firing soon diminished. It appeared that the attack was only a blind, and that the insurgents were trying to burn down the Residency gate going out to cantonments, which was an unsuccessful move on their part. Reported this morning that a number of men, hackeries, and camels, were going over the bridge of boats, perhaps the king going off. Soap is become so scarce an article now that little square pieces are selling for seven rupees!!! Paid our servants to-day one month's wages, minus a rupee each. Two artillerymen wounded to-day. C. and T. went, after dinner, to look at the place where the wall in the ladies' room had fallen in.

Tuesday, September 8th.

HEARD a good deal of firing during the night, and more bullets fell in our court-yard than have ever done before. Some of the bricks of the wall also came down. We thought we saw some one in the bath-rooms in the night and were all frightened, and sent the punkah Coolie to see who it was, but it turned out to be the shadow of our own figures in the moonlight. Got a present yesterday of three pieces of soap from Dr. Scott. I forgot to mention that on Saturday last an officer committed suicide by shooting himself. Captain Simons (Artillery) died this morning.

Mrs. Inglis and I looked into the ladies' square in the evening. It seemed very wretched and miserable. Nearly all the ladies

have moved out of it. We were saying to each
other yesterday, how surprised people in England would be to hear how long we have been
without bread, butter, vegetables, or eggs. Now
and then one or two of the latter are procured
for eight annas or one rupee each!!! *Many*
people without milk or sugar, and all seem to
be suffering from a scarcity of soap, which is
worse than all, *I* think.   A dhoby came this
morning and said he would wash our things
for ten rupees (1*l.*) the dozen, but without
ironing them, and of course without starch
and soap; so, as we can wash quite as well
ourselves, we declined his services. We shall
soon be reduced to our last cake of soap!

Wednesday, September 9th.

WE blew up one of the enemy's mines this morning. The shock was very severe, and made much noise in our court-yard, as a good deal of plaster and mud fell down; a piece of a shell fell close to our door. None of our people were hurt, but I do not believe the explosion was so successful as was expected. It took place while we were at breakfast.

Captain Carnegie came and told Colonel Inglis this evening that the insurgents are fighting among themselves, and that they will not let the king go away from this. That he has not paid his troops, and that they are desirous of coming to terms with us, and even talk of a flag of truce; but it is evident that not the least reliance can be placed on these reports. All, however, are unanimous in thinking that the enemy are getting disheartened, and well they may, as hitherto they have been unsuccessful in everything they have undertaken. A great number of people seen about this evening.

Thursday, September 10th.

THERE was a good deal of firing during the night, and at times there has been a good deal this morning. The brass gun, which one would say was actually firing into our courtyard, is something dreadful in sound, and shakes one's whole frame. Nothing particular going on to-day. Carry and I walked for a long time this evening in the adjoining court-yard, and as there had been some very heavy rain previously, we found it cool and pleasant.

Friday, September 11th.

THIS morning at eleven o'clock we blew up one of the enemy's mines. It appears to have been very successful, but I believe there were several of the wretched creatures outside very badly wounded. The shock was extremely severe, and if Colonel Inglis had not insisted on every one of us remaining inside, some one would most likely have been killed by the large masses of brick-work which fell close to our door. The whole court-yard was full of them, and of branches of the trees which were knocked off in the crash. Carry has been washing all the morning, but it has been so rainy and windy that the things have all got wet again. Dr. Scott came this evening to see the children.

Saturday, September 12th.

Two men of the 32nd were wounded yesterday. A second mine, somewhere near the church, was blown up by our people in the afternoon of yesterday, also with success. Poor little Johnny was very unwell last night. As all the three children are ill, our room is more like a hospital than any thing else. Just as we were in the midst of dressing, washing, and having our room swept out, an old Frenchwoman, to whom we had given some clothes before the siege began, came to see us, and asked for some tea and old clothes, if we had any to give her, as she had lost those we had given her; but of course nothing of that kind do we possess beyond what we have for daily use.

Sunday, September 13th.

LAST night a grassent belonging to the insurgents came in, and we read his deposition. He states our force to be 4000 strong and a regiment of Sikhs, and that they crossed the river on this side of Cawnpore four days ago ; that Maun Sing is at Chinhut, waiting orders from our troops ; that hitherto he had remained neutral, waiting, no doubt, to see which side will be victorious. If this be true it is good news for us, and I do trust ten days more will see our relief in Lucknow. Colonel Inglis appears more sanguine than I have yet seen him since the siege began. Captain Mansfield (32nd) was seized with cholera last night about twelve o'clock, and died before twelve this morning,

As a man and an officer he will be universally
regretted.   Alas, the poor 32nd! how few
remain now.

Monday, September 14th.

WE hear that there is a great deal of
excitement in the city to-day, and that a
good many people are to be seen about this
place.   I believe that an attack is anticipated
to-morrow.   A man came in to-day from
outside, supposed to be a spy.   He represents himself as being the servant of some
lady in the garrison.   His story is that our
reinforcements have *not* crossed the river.
He says that there is to be an attack to-
morrow, at least he had heard so, and that
the Nana is here.

K

Tuesday, September 15th.

CAPTAIN HUTTON, of the Engineers, was killed last evening about seven, on the top of Mr. Gubbins's house.   He will be a dreadful loss, as he was most useful and active in his duties, and was very much liked.   Mrs. Inglis and I went to see Mrs. Pearce yesterday evening.   The weather is very *hot* now ; Johnny not so well to-day; we have all colds, and most people are looking very ill. A man of the 32nd killed to-day, and one wounded.   Little firing, and the day passed off very quietly.   Heard yesterday that some men had been cutting a hole to get at the Treasury.   I spoke to one of the drummers' wives of the 48th in the next square this evening, and she told me that she had heard that the murders at Cawnpore had been most brutal; that little children had been cut up and their bodies stuck on poles. One man, whose name she mentioned, they had tortured horribly; and had asked him, while they were killing him, " How he would like his mutton chops and bread and butter now?" She also says it is reported that these savages have murdered every Christian resident in Lucknow.

Wednesday, September 16th.

DAY very quiet. A letter is to be sent off to our relieving force to-night, and if the messenger brings an answer he is to be most handsomely paid. We hear that there is a native report to the effect that Maun Sing as well as the Nana is here, that he has been ordered here by our force, and if such is the case it would lead us to be-

lieve that they are not far off. They also
say that the insurgents wanted him to join
them, and his reply was that he would show
them how to take the place if they would
give him up one side to himself, but this
they refused to do, fearing he might be in
league with us.

Thursday, September 17th.

SCARCELY any firing during the day, but at
about six o'clock this evening one of our
own shells burst, and the pieces came back
into the ladies' square, killing one child and
wounding another, and also wounding two
poor sweepers, one in the foot and the other
in the hand. I saw the latter pass through
our courtyard to the hospital, supported by
two men, and he seemed to bear his pain
wonderfully. A 32nd man was killed at the
church by a round shot this evening.

Mrs. Inglis bought some coffee yesterday, and is to pay three rupees (6s.) a pound for it ; tea is selling at *sixteen shillings per pound!* I went to see Mrs. Cooper this evening, and Carry and Mrs. Inglis went to see Mrs. Radclyffe.

Friday, September 18th.

LAST night, about twelve o'clock, there was some heavy firing, but it soon subsided. This morning, while we were dressing, one of the enemy's shells or shrapnells burst, and brought down a quantity of brick in our court-yard, pieces of which hit the khansamah and ayah's boy, touching them, however, very slightly. At eleven A.M. there was a partial eclipse of the sun. Gave some of our clothes to a dhoby to wash ; he charges fourteen rupees per hundred, without soap or starch! An enormous piece of wood, three feet three inches in circumference, and thirteen inches long, was sent over the house and fired into the ladies' square this afternoon. No one could believe such a large mass could have come in in that way, unless they actually saw it. It is now supposed that the insurgents have 18 and 32 pounders. Carry and I walked for some time this evening in the next square, but were driven in by a bullet falling near us.

Saturday, September 19th.

NOTHING worth noting has taken place. The day has been quieter than usual. Captain Mansfield's things were sold to-day, prices enormous, 55 rupees for an old flannel shirt; 21 rupees for one bottle of brandy! I think people are desponding and dispirited at getting no news from our force.   It would almost seem as if they had neglected us al-together, and forgotten that such a place as Lucknow exists in the world.

Sunday, September 20th.

HEAVY firing last night, and the guns sounded fearfully loud.   To-day, while Mrs. Inglis and Carry were at church a piece of shell fell deep into the ground close to the cook-room.   Most fortunately none of the servants were sitting there at the time. Carry went to see Mrs. Polehampton this evening.

Monday, September 21st.

A GOOD deal of heavy firing again last night. A bandsman of the 32nd was killed to-day. Several bullets have fallen in our court-yard. It began to rain before daylight this morning, and continued till three P.M. Evening quite cool and pleasant. Heard to-day for the first time that Mrs. Green was dead. She died three weeks ago.

Tuesday, September 22nd.

VERY heavy rain last night; it poured down into our room, and we were obliged to get up and move the boxes and chairs, &c., to

another part of the room. It continued
without ceasing till three P.M., so our room
became like a lake. Everything is damp
and wretched-looking. Some desertions have
occurred to-day; some grassents went away
this morning, and some mess cooks in the
evening. In consequence of the rain there
has been little firing.   Mr. Cunliffe, of
the Artillery, died to-day from fever. He
had been ill some weeks.

Wednesday, September 23rd.

WHEN Colonel Inglis came this morning, he
brought us the delightful intelligence that
his messenger had returned from our reinforcements during the night, and brought a
letter from General Outram, who is coming
here in command of the force. His letter

K 5

was dated 20th September, and stated that they had nearly all crossed the river, and hoped to be with us very shortly. Indeed, had it not been for the very heavy rain we have had the last two days, they might have been here to-day. As it is we hope they will arrive by Sunday next. The force is said to consist of five European and one Sikh regiment. Captain Hardinge also got a letter from his cousin, who is with the advancing troops, and says that a great many regiments are on their way out from England, and that the sensation which all this terrible business has caused at home is something tremendous. The Crimean War, he says, was nothing to it. The Madras Presidency all quiet. In the Bombay, a few disturbances on a small scale.

We cannot be sufficiently thankful to find that our relief is so near, though no doubt there will still be some hard fighting before they reach the Residency gates. A round-shot, a thirty-two pounder, came into our court to-day, knocking down a great piece of the wall, and lodging in the top of an archway. A bullet fell *close* to where Azaib was sitting. Spoke to Dr. and Mrs. Brydon this evening, as they passed through on their way to see Mrs. Cooper.

Thursday, September 24th.

DISTANT guns have been heard during the day, but whether they are our reinforcements or the insurgents fighting among themselves, nobody knows. Some say they sound nearer than yesterday, and that even the smoke was seen. They have been firing a good deal into our courtyard. Two round shots came

in, and the hall has been more knocked
about during the last two days than during
the whole siege.   Mrs. Cooper moved back
into her friend's room yesterday evening.

Friday, September 25th.

WHAT a day is this to be remembered for
life with gratitude towards our Heavenly
Father, for his great mercies, by all those who
have lived through this siege!   Our relief
has arrived!   Firing was heard all day, and
at times very heavy.   About noon our force
was entering the city, and at four P.M.
the firing in the direction of the old band-
stand was said to be very loud, though we
did not hear it in our courtyard.   At six
we were sitting outside our door, when cheers
were heard; great excitement prevailed; servants and soldiers passed by at the most rapid

pace, and Ellicock came up to us looking as pale as a sheet from excitement, and saying that some of the troops had at last arrived at the Residency. They consist, I believe, of the 78th Highlanders, and some of the Madras Fusiliers, besides Artillery; Sir James Outram and General Havelock both with them. They left Cawnpore on the 18th, and their losses coming here have been *very severe.* We hear that they have had 500 killed (a good many officers), and a number of wounded have been brought in. They have come up without tents through all the heavy rain, and with scarcely any provisions. The insurgents had cut trenches in the streets, and loop-holed the houses, so that they could fire down upon them, and shoot them like dogs. It is described as having been a most *murderous* affair!

The bodies of two young ladies were seen lying dead in the street, as if just killed, but

who they were, or where they came from, I
cannot learn.   Sir James Outram has been
slightly wounded.   I have also heard that the
young king who was placed on the throne
a short time ago has been wounded.   The
rest of the force are expected in to-morrow.
Captain Radclyffe has been badly wounded in
the arm to-day.

The horrors these brutal wretches committed at Cawnpore are beyond description. Two officers only, we hear, escaped, *all
the rest, with the women and children*, were
butchered in the most fearful manner; many,
while their bodies were still warm, were
thrown into a place which was used in the
barracks as a bath for the women.   Little
children of all ages were *cut up* into pieces
and roasted before their parents' eyes; and
poor old Sir Hugh Wheler was treated in
some horrible way after they had killed him.
Such would have been our fate, had it not

pleased a God of Mercy to send us relief in time. The noise and excitement consequent on the arrival of the troops is dreadful; and how we shall get any sleep I know not.

CHAP. X.

Saturday, September 26th.

GENERAL HAVELOCK breakfasted with us
this morning, and said he considered their
losses yesterday must have been nearer 600
than 500. Brigadier Neill was killed by
one of the last shots fired. The servants
and natives were looting all day long and
bringing in all kinds of things. Mr. Birch
tells us that the scene outside is beyond
description. Bullocks, camels, baggage of
all description, and wounded men, being
brought in ; natives and soldiers plundering
all they can lay their hands on. Ellicock
says it is more like Donnybrook Fair than
any thing else.

The 90th Regiment have been trying hard all day to make their way in, and every available man in the garrison (all the 32nd I believe) has gone to their assistance. They will encounter great difficulty in getting the baggage and ammunition across the river. The latter is to be brought over on camels, and orders are given that two Europeans are to be at the head of each camel as they cross, to prevent accidents. This has been a sad day from the great anxiety entertained about the safety of the remainder of the force. The casualties are expected to be very numerous. Three mines were discovered to-day, which the enemy were just prepared to blow up. Colonel Campbell of the 90th, who was wounded yesterday, was brought into Colonel Inglis's room just before dinner, and is to remain there, as it will be quieter. The scene while we were at dinner to-day, the appearance of the room, and the whole circumstances, we can never forget! Mr. Thornhill is badly wounded, also Mr. Joly (32nd) and Captain Hughes, who is attached to them, yesterday. I dread to hear of the casualties there will have been to-day. Colonel Inglis has been appointed to the vacant Brigade. He has dearly earned any honours to which he may succeed by all the wear and tear and responsibility he has undergone during this dreadful siege.

Sunday, September 27th.

AFTER all this has been a very painful day; every one is depressed, and all feel that we are in fact *not relieved.* The fighting men we have are too few for our emergency, and too many for the provisions we have in the garrison. A party went out to-day to try and take some of the enemy's guns (100 of the 5th Fusiliers, 18 of the 32nd, Mr. Warnal commanding). The latter led the sortie; they had three men killed and four wounded, and the Fusiliers one killed and one wounded. Did not take any guns, but spiked two. Captain Barrow called and gave a fearful account of the massacre at Cawnpore, which took place the very day that General Havelock's force marched in to relieve them. Poor Mrs. Moore was the only lady of the 32nd who was *killed*, the others died of the hardships they had to undergo. When the people from Futtyghur arrived there, these savages took all the officers and separated them from their wives. They, poor things, declared that they would die with their husbands, and rushed to them, but they were all with the exception of one torn from them, and shut up in the place where the other women were, after which they were all murdered; and they and all the children, some of them their bodies still warm, were thrown into a well. Horrors indescribable were committed. We saw Dr. Scott this evening; he looked fairly done up, and said he had never been so hard-worked in all his life. He really looked so changed, that I should hardly have known him.

Monday, September 28th.

CAPTAIN HUGHES died this morning, and Mr. Alexander, of the Artillery, was wounded and died in the course of the day. A party was to have been sent out this morning to try again to take the guns, but it is put off till to-morrow. The 90th Regiment, with the baggage, have not yet arrived in the Presidency, but have entrenched themselves about four miles outside the city.

This has been a sad day. I have never felt more weary or more depressed since we

came into this place. I do not know how
we are to get on much longer. An attack
is anticipated to-night. The 32nd and 5th
Fusiliers are the only regiments inside;
the others are located in houses close by.
Saw Mrs. Boileau this evening. I gave up
taking sugar to-day, and we are using our
last piece of soap.

Tuesday, September 29th.

AWOKE this morning about four o'clock, and
saw the party assemble in our court to go out
and take the guns. It made my heart sad to
see them, knowing that so many of the poor
fellows would not return alive. They started
shortly before five, composed of parties from
the different regiments here, the brave, gallant 32nd, as usual, leading, commanded
by Mr. M'Cabe, who has distinguished

himself greatly.   This was the fourth sortie
he has led, and is his last, for he fell mortally wounded, and cannot live through the
day.   He will be a great loss, for he was a
right good officer ; had got his commission
for bravery, and now he has died a soldier's
death.   The   party   returned   about   ten
o'clock.   They took seven guns, most of
which had on previous occasions been spiked
by the 32nd.   Mr. Lucas was mortally
wounded, Mr. Edmonstone slightly, and
the officer commanding the 5th Fusiliers
was killed.   The total amount of killed and
wounded we have not yet heard.   The 32nd
behaved, as they always do, *nobly*.   We hear
that Colonel Brooke has exchanged with a
colonel from the Guards, who is supposed
to be at Calcutta by this time.

Captain Moore's poor old faithful khitmaghar came to see us this morning, and con-
firmed all we had heard of the horrors of the

Cawnpore massacre. He remained with them to the last. Captain Moore was killed in the boat in which the treacherous Nana agreed to allow them to escape, and Mrs. Moore was taken out and confined with all the other ladies, women and children. The hardships they underwent were fearful. The only food they had was rice and dhal. Many ladies died before they got out of the fort, and those who survived to that time were all murdered. The poor old khitmaghar was himself imprisoned, and the rope to hang him was actually round his neck, but he contrived to escape. Two days before she was killed, poor Mrs. Moore gave him a letter to her friends in England, and Captain Moore's picture, to try and send home if he could. They were found on his person, and torn before his face into atoms.

The gallantry of the devoted 32nd in the affair of to-day, as well as throughout the whole siege, is now the topic of conversation. One man of the regiment, Webster by name, went out alone and spiked one of the guns. Mr. Edmonstone behaved nobly. I hear they talk of carrying the stone bridge to-morrow or next day, on which occasion the 32nd are again to lead the way, Colonel Inglis himself going out, I believe, with them.

Our rations are to be reduced from to-morrow, wine and beer are nearly all finished, and we shall have to grind our own " attah." Nothing seems to be settled as to what is to be done about the sick and wounded, and women and children. Mrs. Gall came to see us this evening, and I found that they had often, like ourselves, consulted together as to whether it would be wrong to put an end to our own lives if the insurgents were to get in. Different opinions entertained on the subject.

Wednesday, September 30th.

THIS has been a very quiet day. Nothing particular going on. Colonel Inglis has been very unwell, and not able to leave his room. Weather very hot. Heard this evening that there is a report that Nana Sing has been murdered. This is not unlikely if he wished to declare himself on our side. Captain Hardinge is going to-night on what must be a very dangerous expedition. He proposes to go with his Sikhs to the place where the remainder of our force are with the baggage, four miles from this, in a garden on the Cawnpore road, and to try and establish some communication between them and this place. I trust he will return in safety, for he is a brave, good officer;

but the risk seems great when we think of the sad fate that has attended so many who have gone out on similar expeditions.

Thursday, October 1st.

COLONEL INGLIS better this morning. Captain Hardinge could not get out to Allumbagh with his Sikhs last night. They were fired on as soon as they were seen, and obliged to come back and give up the attempt. I spoke to a man who came in with the force from Cawnpore; he is a tailor, belonging to the regiment. He gave an alarming account of the *numbers* outside; he said he thought that there were about 100,000 men about this place, and that the Nana is with them. He had seen our poor old bungalows, and says that they are occupied by sepoys. I could hear nothing of our servants from him.

A party of men from different regiments started to-day, about four P.M., to take possession of some houses near this. They have not yet returned, but, I believe, have been getting on well, and we have just heard they have taken one of the Bazaars. So I hope some provisions may be procured. Mrs. Inglis bought half-a-pound of common sugar to-day, for which she gave four rupees! We spoke to Mr. Browne, Mr. Foster, and Captain Bessano, as they were standing in our court with their mess. They tell us that there are now only four officers and about 250 men of the 32nd fit for duty. Alas! the poor 32nd; how I grieve to think of them.

At this present time, there are 800 wounded in this garrison, and 410 women and children. When we do get away, what an undertaking it will be! Mr. M'Cabe died this morning. Poor Captain Radclyffe is sinking fast. Mrs. Cooper's baby died this evening. Mrs. Inglis's baby has been ill to-day.

Friday, October 2nd.

POOR Captain Radclyffe died last night, about half-past ten. A party went out this morning and got possession of some of the enemy's guns. I believe they have now no guns just round the Residency. They took them away last night, while they made a feigned attack. The firing, to us, sounded loud and near. When our men went out, on Tuesday, to take the guns, two of them (one 32nd and the other Madras Fusiliers) fell into a well, and there remained till this morning. The former was killed, but not the latter, who, however, was afraid to call out, till he heard European voices go by. They threw him a rope down and pulled him up, none the worse, only suffering, as may be supposed, from the most ravenous hunger. Truly he had a wonderful escape!

Saturday, October 3rd.

A VERY quiet day; scarcely a shot fired. There appears to be a perfect stagnation of every thing; but I suppose they must be doing something towards advancing matters. Distant guns have been heard in the direction of Allumbagh, where the force with the baggage are. They have with them 250 fighting men, and provisions for the whole force here for a fortnight. Everything is now getting very scarce : sugar, almost impossible to be got for any price ; 25 rupees was offered to-day for a seer (2 lbs.), and without success; 25 rupees for one bottle of brandy. Mrs. Inglis bought some soap; 4 rupees for a very small cake of *common* brown! I got one of my boxes from the Residency; it was so knocked about by shot and shell—having formed a barricade—that I should not have recognised it, and every thing inside was ruined. To-morrow I am going to examine another through which a round shot has been.

We certainly have been very unfortunate as regards our things; but I would have cared for nothing, could I but have preserved my Bombay box with all my precious letters and William's picture. But all are gone, and regrets will not recall them.

Sunday, October 4th.

READ the Colonel's despatch, which is going to be sent to Calcutta. It gives a very clear and good account of the whole siege. Went to Morning Service, and received the Holy Communion. Afterwards I went to see Mrs. Radclyffe, who looked very ill. Poor thing! how I feel for her! This has been a quiet day, till about nine P.M., when the enemy made some noise; and four bullets fell in our court-yard in a very short space of time.

Monday, October 5th.

A MOST flattering Order published by Sir James Outram about the manner in which this

garrison has been defended by Colonel Inglis
and the officers and men under his command.
The whole affair he describes as being unparalleled in the annals of history. I hope
Colonel Inglis is certain of being made a
K.C.B. A letter has been received to-day
from the troops at Allumbagh. They had
made a sortie, and had got in some provisions. Ours are rapidly diminishing; and
to-day we have begun to restrict ourselves
to two chupatties each a day; and soon, I
fear, we shall have to eat horseflesh; but
as yet we have beef and rice. I have been
hungry to-day, and could have eaten more,
had I had it. Seven men and three officers
came in to-day from the Fureed Bux, badly
wounded. Mrs. Roberts came to see us this
morning, and told us the chloroform at the
hospital is all gone. Mrs. Omiley's two children both died in one hour a day or two ago.

Tuesday, October 6th.

THIS morning, between eight and nine A.M., the enemy blew up a mine, and commenced an attack which lasted nearly three hours. They regained the position which our people had got possession of yesterday. A serjeant of the 32nd was killed and one man wounded, and two of the 90th slightly injured in the explosion. From what I heard, it appears that the attack had more plan and system in it than the former ones. I went this evening to see Mrs. Radclyffe. We had a visit from Mrs. Giddings.

Wednesday, October 7th.

OUR people have been blowing up houses this morning. Little firing during the early part of the day ; but between five and six o'clock, just as we were sitting down to dinner, the enemy commenced a heavy fire on the Cawnpore Battery, and they have been pounding away ever since till the hour I am now writing — nine P. M. I got 100 rupees to-day from Mr. Giddings, and gave the servants a little money each towards their wages; Azaib and Din Mahomet have had 18 rupees each, and the two Coolies eight each. Mrs. Cooper came to see us in the afternoon. The weather still continues very warm.

Thursday, October 8th.

A QUIET day. Heard that 250 men and twenty cartloads of provisions had reached Allumbagh yesterday from Cawnpore. Decidedly our people in the garrison seem in a brighter mood to-day, and talk of the strong force coming up, and which is said to be now between Calcutta and Cawnpore; though the general opinion is that a month at least must elapse before more troops will be here. Captain Barrow came to see us to-day. He said that from the time they left Cawnpore up to this date there have been 24 officers and 240 men killed, and 44 officers and 772 men wounded.

A man of the 32nd, while walking out near some of the works this morning, saw something like a garment of some kind lying on the ground, and on going to pick it up, found two bags of rupees, each containing 500 rupees. An easy way of making 100*l*.

Captain and Mrs. Orr came to see us this evening. Mr. Edmonstone also paid us a long visit. He told us that he had heard a report had gone to England some time ago that our garrison here had been cut to pieces! Mrs. Orr mentioned a very narrow escape she had some time ago. She was sitting on a chair outside her door, and was in the act of leaning forward to pick up something for her child, when a round shot came in and broke the chair she was sitting on, without touching her. A gentleman, a few days ago, had half his pillow carried off by a round shot whilst he was lying on it, and it did not even awake him. These wonderful escapes are so frequent here that one hears them related without feeling much astonishment; but I think that should we ever find ourselves once again in safety, and able calmly to reflect over what we have heard and seen during the siege, it will surprise even our own selves.

Friday, October 9th.

DAY quiet. Mr. Cromelin, of the Engineers, whom we formerly knew at Peshawur, came to see us. A letter has been received by Sir James Outram this evening from the officer commanding at Cawnpore, stating " that Delhi has positively fallen at last; that our losses there have been sixty-one officers and 2000 men killed and wounded; that they have had an addition to their force at Cawnpore of 300 men; and that at Allumbagh they have now 500 men, and have been able to go out and scour the country and get in some provisions." There is a report in the garrison that Maun Sing has offered to take charge of the sick and wounded and women and children, if a force is sent out from this, but I cannot vouch for the truth of it, nor do I think, after all the treachery we have heard of on the part of the natives, that many would be anxious to entrust themselves to his care, though he has saved the lives of some ladies, whose names I have heard mentioned.

Saturday, October 10th.

THE more this siege is talked of, the more wonderful does it appear how the insurgents around us have been kept at bay so long, when our garrison was so weak and our position was such a bad one. At one time we were so much in want of artillerymen, that the men who manned the guns had actually to run from one to the other as they were required to load and fire. We heard that at one time the enemy had made a breach large enough for a regiment to march in in perfect order, and yet they did not take advantage of it. It appears quite marvellous. Maun Sing has been wounded they say. An attack seems to be anticipated to-night; and all the sentries are to be doubled. A good many people have been seen to-day about the bridge of boats. More going away than coming in. Several artillery horses, all harnessed but without guns, came in this direction. Dr. Scott came while we were at dinner, and mentioned the names of several people who had died or were killed at Delhi; amongst them, Brigadiers Halifax and Reid, General Barnard, Colonel Chester, and others whom I cannot remember; but their losses have been small in comparison to ours since the relieving force left Cawnpore.

CHAP. XI.

Sunday, October 11th, 1857.

This has been a quieter day than usual. We went to Divine Service in the morning. The enemy blew up two mines, but, as usual, they were unsuccessful, though a soldier of the 78th was killed by one. Mrs. Brydon came to see us this evening, and gave us a melancholy account of the death of Captain Beecher (of the Artillery) who was wounded in the arm coming in with the Relieving Force, and died of lock-jaw. She also gave us a sad description of three days at the Gubbins's, when Mrs. Dorin and Major Banks were killed, and Captains Forbes and

Grant wounded in the early part of the siege,
also Dr. Brydon, while sitting at the dinner
table.   It made one's heart sick to listen to
the sad details.

Monday, October 12th.

LAST night letters from Major Bruce, at
Cawnpore, were brought in by a messenger.
They stated that a force from Delhi was moving up towards this place, and was expected to
be at Alleyghur on the 5th instant, which
would bring them to Cawnpore about the
20th.   More troops are arriving every day
at the latter place.   Captain and Mrs. Barwell came to see us this evening.   Mrs. Inglis
has been writing a very tiny letter to her
family, and a messenger has been found who,
I believe, will take it out this evening.   It is
addressed to Brigadier Wilson, at Cawnpore,

who is to forward it to Colonel Birch, at
Calcutta.   I trust it may arrive safely, as at
such a time news will be beyond any price to
those who have friends here.

Tuesday, October 13th.

DAY very quiet.   No news of any kind.
The mornings and evenings are now delight-
fully cool, but the days hot.   Mr. Thornhill died yesterday afternoon.   The enemy
have been so quiet during the last few days,
that they must be meditating plans of mischief, and when they do make another attack
I fear it will be a sharp one.   Captain Barrow,
Mrs. Giddings, and Mrs. Orr came to see
us this evening.

Wednesday, October 14th.

ANOTHER quiet day; the enemy made a *demonstration* last night, and fired a good deal. While we were at breakfast this morning a message was brought to Colonel Inglis, reporting that some Sikhs from outside were anxious to come in, and wished to know whether they would be pardoned if they go out and fight on our side with the force which is coming up. The reply given them by Captain Harding, was to "go and do their best." Maun Sing has made an offer to protect us all and fight on our side, if the authorities decide on coming to terms with him, which if they did would, probably, end in our being sent off sooner than we at present expect; but I should feel very doubtful and suspicious of even Maun Sing's promises now, after the fatal Cawnpore business; I fear there is treachery somewhere! Poor Mr. Harmer came to see us this evening, walking on crutches, and looking very different from the fresh rosy boy he was when at Kurrachee with us,. just out from England, little more than twenty months ago! I fear he will always be lame. It made me quite sad to see him. Mrs. Giddings, Mrs. Orr, and Mrs. Boileau passed through our square this evening. Colonel Inglis sent his tiny English note off at last, addressed to Brigadier Wilson, at Cawnpore.

Thursday, October 15th.

ANOTHER quiet day. Colonel Inglis brought us some *beautiful* jewels to show us. An old pensioner who came to see Colonel Inglis this evening, talked much over the present state of affairs.   He mentioned the names of some of the great men who are fighting against us. Captain Barrow came while he was here, and acted as interpreter.   I have been so lame all day that I can scarcely put my foot to the ground.

Friday, October 16th.

I BELIEVE an attack was expected to-day, but up to this hour (nine P.M.) all has been quiet. Caroline went to see Mrs. Polehampton and Mrs. Gall and Mrs. Barber this evening.   The evenings and mornings are quite cold now, and I think it is very chilly with the punkah.

Saturday, October 17th.

A GREAT deal of firing last night, but it does not appear that the enemy did any mischief, though from the sound, round shot and bullets seemed to fall close to our court-yard. No news of any kind to-day, except that distant guns were heard yesterday. Heard the bagpipes this evening for the first time.

Sunday, October 18th.

CARRY and I attended Divine Service this morning. Three men came in from Cawnpore last night; they say troops are coming in every day to that place. The 93rd and 23rd Regiments, and four troops of Horse Artillery are on their way from Calcutta. A Sikh came in with a message from Maun Sing, saying that he had always served our government and still wished to do so; that he was willing to withdraw and that he would protect us and give us assistance whenever our force marched out of this place, but that he has only 10,000 men that he can positively depend upon.

Mrs. Giddings came to see us this evening; she does not appear the worse for the siege, but looks in better health and is better dressed than any one I see. We have been out of soap for some days and are now obliged to wash with what is called "bason" (ground grain made into a paste with water). It is a nice clean thing, and the best substitute for soap.

Monday, October 19th.

A "HOME NEWS" was brought in last night from Allumbagh, date "26th August." Quite an event, and every one in the garrison most anxious of course to have a look at it.

We got it here for an hour. They had heard, in England, of Sir Henry Lawrence's death, but do not appear to have had any account of the Cawnpore massacre or Lucknow siege, as no mention is made of either. Got in some sugar and, I believe, a few other provisions, into the garrison last night. Between eleven and twelve last night the enemy commenced one of their unmeaning attacks. The musketry was very sharp indeed for a short time, but they did us no mischief.

A letter has been sent from Sir James Outram to Maun Sing to-day, but the contents I have not heard. Probably it tends rather to negotiating; and to have him as an ally would no doubt be a great thing for us, as we should then be enabled to get in provisions for the sick and wounded, who are very badly off for every thing. I am so lame from an inflamed foot that I can scarcely walk a step. Captain Barrow came to see us this evening. I went to see Mrs. Radclyffe. In consequence of Colonel Inglis having laid in a small store of provisions, we are better off than most people in the way of food, but beef, rice, dhal, and chupatties are the only eatables ever seen now, and even a small quantity of sugar coming into the garrison is quite an event. Yesterday, while Johnny and I were walking in the next square, a Sikh officer passing quite close to us, was shot in the arm by a bullet. Captain Barrow had a very narrow escape a few days ago, a bullet passing through his hat without touching him.

Tuesday, October 20th.

A MESSENGER arrived last night from Cawnpore, bringing word that troops were daily

M

coming up to that place. A native reports in the garrison to-day that the Delhi Force is at Futtyghur (seven marches from Cawnpore). A child near the Residency had half its head carried away this morning by the bursting of a shell, and another was badly wounded. Captain Gordon of the 6th Native Infantry, acting here as Judge Advocate General, called on Mrs. Inglis to-day. He had been Aide-de-Camp to General Neill. He told us that at Allahabad fourteen officers, out of seventeen who had sat down to mess, were murdered by their own men, when the sepoys rose there; one poor ensign escaped murder, but died of starvation. Also that the Rajah of Gwalior is not fighting against us, but that he cannot restrain his men, who with thirty-one guns have joined the other mutineers.

I find that Sir Henry Lawrence's death was made known in England by a letter which Mr. Gubbins wrote to the Governor-General very soon after the occurrence. 10 P.M.—We have just heard that a letter has arrived for Sir James Outram, from Maun Sing, and that the purport of it is that Maun Sing will fight for us if he is pardoned and his life spared. He has a force of 10,000 men.

Wednesday, October 21st.

A QUIET night, but a good deal of firing this morning. When Colonel Inglis came to breakfast, he told us that a young boy (an apothecary belonging to the 32nd) was killed by a round shot while asleep in his bed at the hospital this morning, poor fellow!

From what we hear, Maun Sing appears to

have made strong professions of his willingness to assist us, in his letter of last night, and negotiating with him will, probably, be the order of the day. Much confidence does not seem to be placed in any good that he can do us, for they say he has very little power, and the fidelity of his followers, when once he joins us, is, after all, doubtful.

What a state this country is in. Scarcely a native regiment has remained entirely true to us, and every day one hears some new tale of horror of the past massacres which makes one's heart sicken. The enemy blew up two mines to-day, but did no harm. One of the 78th had both his legs taken off by a round shot while standing in a room, talking to some of his comrades. I went to see Mrs. Radclyffe this evening, and found Mrs. Clarke with her, who told me some more dreadful things about the poor people

at Cawnpore, which she had heard from one
of the two officers who alone escaped from
that fatal place.

Thursday, October 22nd.

DISTANT guns and musketry were heard this
morning while we were dressing; supposed
to be the enemy making an attack on Allumbagh.   It did not appear to last very long.
A quantity of shawls, chiefly Umritsur manu-
facture, were brought for us to look at.   I did
not see one I admired.   Mrs. Pearce came in
the evening to show us her baby, and Mrs.
Need brought in her children.   Some people
complain of the want of provisions, but most
seem to have enough, though, of course, no
variety; and I must say, I am beginning to
get very tired of beef and rice every day for
so long.   I am more weary than I can ever

express of this sad captivity. I feel at times so melancholy.

Friday, October 23rd.

No news to-day of any kind, except the pleasing intelligence that we are better supplied with food than was supposed, and now they say we can hold out for thirty-three days longer as regards provisions. A great sale has been going on in the brigade mess-room. We hear that two bottles of champagne have been sold for twelve rupees each, and a bottle of brandy, thirty rupees! Three rupees can be got any day for *one cigar*. Mr. Charlton paid us a visit this evening; he looks dreadfully ill, and very weak. Mrs. Giddings also called this evening, and Mrs. Cooper came in just as we had finished dinner.

Saturday, October 24th.

THIS morning, at breakfast, Colonel Inglis informed us that arrangements had been made that our provisions might last till the 1st of December, and in consequence our rations (with the exception of the meat) are to be reduced to-morrow. They do not appear to think that Maun Sing has any intention of assisting us, in consequence of which we must make up our minds to wait till our relief comes in, and go on as we are now doing. The evident intention of the insurgents is to try and starve us out. Sir J. Outram gave a man the other day 1000 rupees to go and bring in some sugar from some place in one of the enemy's positions; but the man never returned. Colonel Campbell is very unwell to-day. I went to see Mrs. Radclyffe, and found Captain Barrow sitting with Mrs. Inglis when I came back.

Sunday, October 25th.

CARRY and I attended Divine Service and Holy Communion this morning. Maun Sing's vakeel came in with a message from his master, the particulars of which I have not heard. Captain Wilson, Colonel Napier, and Captain Birch, came to drink tea with us yesterday evening, which was quite an event in our quiet life. Mrs. Inglis has been suffering a good deal from her foot, but her patience is wonderful.

Monday, October 26th.

A MESSENGER came in last night with the news that a force, under Colonel Greathed of H.M. 8th Regiment, had gone out from Agra, had an engagement with the enemy, beaten them, and taken twelve of their guns; and also had had a fight with the rebels at Bithoor. Troops are said to be coming in every day to Cawnpore from Calcutta. Heard to-day that Maun Sing had proposed having an underground passage into this place, that he and his followers might come in and out as they liked ; by no means a pleasant idea !

At times, how very dark and gloomy our prospects appear. Now that the insurgents are getting well beaten at Delhi and elsewhere, I fear they will all make for this place. A good many sepoys have been seen to-day coming over the bridge, and it was remarked, as an unusual thing, that they stopped and spoke to those they met going out. The enemy have been getting two guns into position this evening to bear upon the Brigade Mess. It is thought that they will do us a great deal of mischief. As expected, our rations have been reduced to-day, with the exception of the meat. We are now commencing on two attah chupatties each a day, and two made of *gram* between us all. I am more distressed about the want of soap than anything else. The weather just now is very pleasant, and a punkah quite unnecessary, except to keep off the mosquitoes at night. Mrs. Cooper came in for a few minutes to-day, and appeared very desponding about the reduction of the provisions. Colonel Campbell called to-day : he has been improving ever since Dr. Scott took him in hand.

Tuesday, October 27th.

ANOTHER messenger came in last night with a letter for Sir James Outram. Five hundred men with provisions have arrived at Allumbagh, and 1000 more troops at Cawnpore, so that altogether the news is good, though at times our little garrison seems depressed. It is reported that a good many of the Delhi rebels have gone to their homes, which I hope is true, and then we shall not have them adding to the numbers against us here. Captain Barrow came for a few minutes this afternoon.

At eight P.M. this evening another messenger from Maun Sing came in, but not the man they wanted. Evidently some plan for negotiating is thought of. The messenger who came in states that Miss Jackson and her brother were brought into Lucknow yesterday in irons! and are under the care of Maun Sing, who has hitherto protected them. Poor young girl! who knows what misery and suffering she may have undergone. Her fate, with that of her brother and sister, has caused great interest ever since the commencement of the outbreak in the district. I have not heard what has become of her sister, but no doubt some diplomatic reason has caused Maun Sing to bring these two individuals to Lucknow just now. Mr. Graydon (44th Native Infantry) has been mortally wounded to-day. A very good officer, and a great loss he will be, Colonel Inglis says.

Wednesday, October 28th.

NEWS came in last night that the force from Delhi has arrived at Cawnpore. Another messenger in to-day from Maun Sing. He said that his master did not like to send the man we wanted, as he fears to risk his life coming in. I suppose he is one of his chiefs. He says Maun Sing is ready to obey General Havelock's orders, and will send in another man to-morrow. I hear there are some other fugitives with Sir M. Jackson and his sister — Captain Orr's brother among the number. It seems that they have not been under Maun Sing's protection, but that he has offered large bribes to get them made over to him. If the general comes to terms with Maun Sing it may perhaps enable us all to get away from this place

sooner than we at present expect. Mrs.
Inglis better to-day, and Dr. Scott has
not paid us his usual visit. Mr. Birch came
and sat with us for a short time after dinner.
I went over to speak to Colonel Campbell
this afternoon, and was glad to find him
better.

Thursday, October 29th.

A MESSENGER came in this morning from
Allumbagh. Our troops there have got provisions to last them for some time. The
enemy are constructing a battery close to
them. Some anxiety seems to be felt regarding the Gwalior troops, who, it is thought,
are marching towards Lucknow, having with
them a siege train, so if they were to come
here they would be by no means a pleasant
addition to the numbers outside. The losses

at Delhi have been very great.   I hear sixty-
one officers have been killed and wounded.

Captain Barrow came to see us for a few
minutes to-day : he said he thought our force
might be here on the 10th of next month.
Saw Colonel Campbell for a few minutes
this afternoon.   He is better, but still looks
very ill.

Friday, October 30th.

No news to-day of any kind.   Went to
see Mrs. Cooper this morning, and also
Mrs. Banks.   Saw " The Friend of India "
for a few minutes.   The whole country appears to be in an unsettled and disturbed
state.   Every paper one sees, and all one
hears, tends to confirm this.   The enemy
blew up a mine this morning near the place
where the 78th Highlanders are quartered,

but it fortunately did no harm. Dr. Scott called this evening, just for a few minutes, on his way to Colonel Campbell's.

The state of our garrison here, as regards the 32nd Regiment, in numbers was, on the 29th June 651, and on the 25th September 401! A sad list of killed in all this sad business.

Saturday, October 31st.

A MESSENGER has been in to-day from Maun Sing. He has stated, I believe, that he is willing to withdraw, and the general has given him four days to do so. We shall be anxious to see the result. A letter has been received from Captain Orr's brother; it is signed by all their party, and says that they are well treated, and very happy. It is likely that they may have been forced to write it,

but such, I hope, is not the case, and trust
that their statement is true, poor things.
Several bullets have fallen in our court to-
day. Captain Barrow and Mr. Birch came
this evening, and had some tea with us.
There was a great sale yesterday, and I believe one again to-day.

Sunday, November 1st.

A very quiet day; no news of any kind;
attended Divine Service. Went to see Mrs.
Radclyffe before dinner. Captain Barrow
dined with us. The nights are now most
lovely, and I believe to-night is full moon.
An 18-pound shot went into the Fayrers' house
yesterday, into Mrs. Barwell's room, and hit
the place where she always sits; but most fortunately she was out spending the day with a
friend.

Monday, November 2nd.

THERE have been several casualties to-day; Mr. Grant, an officer of the 41st Native Infantry, and five Europeans and seven Sikhs wounded. A messenger came in from Allumbagh this evening, with a letter stating that Sir Colin Campbell is expected at Cawnpore to-day with an additional force of 1000 men, which, if true, is very good news. He states that a large force of ours is at Bunnee, but that is only a native report. He adds that, as he came through the city, he saw a great many sowars, and they gave him this piece of intelligence; also that the enemy intend making an attack to-night. Captain Birch came and had tea with us.

Our evenings and mornings are now quite

cold.   Got our rations to-day.   If every one gets the same rations we do, I am sure no one need be starving; for *we* have plenty, owing to Mrs. Inglis's good management in always weighing out the exact quantity of attah required for the chupatties we use each day.

Tuesday, November 3rd.

NOTHING particular has been going on to-day.   There was no attack last night.   I do not think Colonel Inglis expects the reinforcements to arrive here before the 20th or 30th.   I talked to Colonel Campbell for a short time this afternoon, and found out that he had known my dear brother when they were together in the Crimea.   Colonel Campbell had command of the party which held the "Quarries" the night of that fatal 8th of June, when dearest William was killed. What a fatal month June has been to me! Mr. Birch came and had tea with us this evening. He told us a good deal about the dreadful doings at Cawnpore, and one tale seems more dreadful than another. Three officers only and one man escaped the massacre. Fifteen Europeans took refuge in a mosque near the river, which the enemy surrounded, and then set fire to the brushwood to prevent their escape. A consultation was held as to what would be best for them to do, when it was found that only three officers and two men could swim; and in order to save these, the remainder of the party agreed to make a sally and create a diversion, and thus enable them to get away. Accordingly, those who could swim, jumped into the water. One officer has since died, and one man was killed in getting away; the others swam down the river six miles, when they saw some natives

who took off their turbans to them, and
laying down their arms, beckoned to the
poor fugitives to come on shore. They did
so, and were taken by these people, who belonged to some Rajah, and treated with
great care and kindness. Captain Moore
appears to have acted through the whole
Cawnpore business with the greatest gallantry.   Distant guns were heard to-day.

CHAP. XII.

Wednesday, November 4th, 1857.

No messenger in last night. One man coming in two nights ago was taken by the insurgents, and two "Home News," which he was bringing with him were lost, which is provoking. As we were sitting down to breakfast this morning, Captain Hardinge came to report that Mr. Dashwood had just had both his legs wounded by a round shot. He has since had them both amputated just above the ancle; and as there is no more chloroform, I fear he must have suffered a great deal, and from having been so long laid up previously it is hardly to be expected that he will get over it.

Caroline and I went to see Mrs. Ogilvie before dinner, and sat with her some time. Mrs. Vokins came to speak to Mrs. Inglis this afternoon about going home with her, but she seems to have changed her intention of going to England.   So Mrs. Inglis will be rather at a loss who to take home as a servant. Two of Colonel Inglis's kids, and a fine large goat of Mrs. Cooper's, were killed by some of the Fusiliers who were on guard. An attack has, I believe, been expected to-day.   A great many people have been seen about the Baillie Gate, but I dare say, as has frequently been the case when any thing of the kind is expected, nothing will come of it.   The days are now getting so short, and the evenings so long, that it is very wearisome and gloomy, and we long more than ever for change of scene and air.

Thursday, November 5th.

THERE was a good deal of musketry fire last night, between nine and ten o'clock. An artilleryman was badly wounded. Colonel Campbell was very unwell indeed this morning, and I fear the doctors have a bad opinion of his case. Colonel Inglis bought some pretty little cups and saucers at the prize agent's to-day, and gave Carry and me each a very pretty cup. Distant guns (supposed to be at Allumbagh) were heard to-day, and there is a report in the garrison that Sir Colin Campbell was at that place, but we hardly believe it. We spoke to Captain Orr to-day. He told us that he had not heard from his brother, who is a prisoner here, since the 30th ult. The letter he then wrote represented them all as being well taken care of, as far as their bodily wants, such as food and clothes, went, but Captain Orr thinks that the letter must have been dictated, as it said so little, and was brought in by one of Maun Sing's men. The party of prisoners consists of Sir Mountstuart Jackson and his sister, Captain and Mrs. Orr, their little girl, six years' old, and a sergeant-major. When they were brought into Lucknow the gentlemen were on a bullock gharry in irons, and the ladies in dooleys. They must have undergone great hardships. I understand that they are now under the care of the king's sepoys. There is a report to-day that Maun Sing has gone away, but I believe no one knows whether such is really the case.

Mrs. Giddings came just before our dinner, and remained some time. She brought some bread which she had made with only attah and water, and it was very good, but I prefer the chupatties to eat every day. We are going to content ourselves with one *attah* chupattie each a day, making out the rest with gram, now that food is becoming more scarce. Poor Mrs. C—— comes to see us every day. She is so desponding and melancholy when she talks of provisions being likely to fail, that it is quite sad to hear her.

Friday, November 6th.

DISTANT guns heard to-day, and musketry reported by the officer on the look out. Maun Sing is reported to have gone to Chinhut, and taken about 3 or 4000 men with him. Major Eyre, of the Artillery, came to see Mrs. Inglis to-day. He told us, among other things, that a conspiracy for taking the fort at Calcutta had been got up by the rebels; for-

tunately, however, without success. It appears
that at the very commencement of the outbreak in Bengal, just before the mutiny at
Barrackpore, the Rajah of Gwalior (generally
called Scindiah) was to have given a magnificent *fête* at Calcutta to the Governor-General
and all the great people there, in some gardens. They were to have had waterworks
and all kinds of amusements, but it was put
off in consequence of a violent hurricane
which came on suddenly. It is stated that
the rebels intended murdering the Governor-
General, and all the people in authority,
and taking possession of the fort. It is supposed that the plan was unknown to the
Rajah, but previously he paid a visit to the
Nana, acknowledging him as Peishwa, which
looked rather suspicious. However, he has
hitherto been favourable to us, and has kept
his men in check longer than it was supposed
he could do.

Colonel Campbell is going on better. I went to see Mrs. Radclyffe before dinner. We were told that some of the soldiers belonging to the new force are so hungry that they will do anything to obtain food, and constantly run into the kitchens whenever they see cooking going on, seize on a chupattie, and leave a rupee in its place!! Poor fellows, it is indeed sad to hear of their being upon guard or duty of some kind all night long, especially now the mornings are so cold and keen, and that without enough to eat.

Saturday, November 7th.

LAST night, just as we were going to bed, We heard that a messenger had arrived from Cawnpore with a letter from Major Bruce, stating that the army commanded by Sir Colin Campbell in person was expected to reach Allumbagh on the 10th instant. It consists of 5100 infantry, 600 cavalry, and 36 guns—a fine force; and if it does not effectually release us, I do not think any thing will. Colonel Inglis appears to think they will reach this place on the 13th, and unless the rebels retreat on their arrival, the women and children and the sick and wounded will have to be sent off at once, taking with us merely a change of clothes, and carrying only what can be taken in bundles in our hands. Those who are able will have to walk to Allumbagh, as all the carriages, buggies, and carts will be occupied by the sick and wounded; it will be a dreadful affair getting us off. Mrs. M'Bean has, I believe, promised to lend Colonel Inglis a palkie gharry and a cart for us all to go in and take our things. It is just possible that the enemy may go away, and affairs may take a better

turn, and we may not have to be hurried off
so rapidly; but at all events, I do not think
there will be much delay in our departure
after the force once comes in. The enemy
blew up a mine this morning, but without
doing any harm. The mornings and evenings are very cold now, and every one is
busy getting warm clothing made up, for
the children especially.

Sunday, November 8th.

COLONEL INGLIS was very unwell this morning, and obliged to send for Dr. Scott after
breakfast. Carry and I attended Divine
Service, and remained for the Communion.
Mr. Browne (32nd) was slightly wounded to-
day. Colonel Campbell not so well, and I do
not think the doctors think favourably of him.
I went to see Mrs. Radclyffe before dinner,

and found her looking forward with dread
and anxiety to our move from Lucknow.   I
am certain it will be a terrible business
getting us all off.   Once at Allumbagh, I
imagine that we shall be over the most difficult part.   Every thing very quiet here to-
day.

Monday, November 9th.

COLONEL INGLIS better this morning, but
had a bad night.   When Dr. Scott came to
see us he said he thought that we should
be away from this before the 20th, and
advised us to begin at once and prepare
for our move.   They say that we shall have
to leave a great many things behind us, which
we never can expect to see again.   We hope
to begin to-morrow and settle a little.   A
great deal of firing has been going on from
the enemy to-day.   Two European artillery-

men and one native were wounded this evening. Captain Barrow came to see Colonel Inglis, and remained to dinner with us, which he seemed to enjoy, for he had made a very early dinner; and though people may have *enough,* no one seems to have too much to eat just now. We have not seen Colonel Inglis, as he has been confined to his room all day.

Tuesday, November 10th.

COLONEL INGLIS better to-day, but not able to breakfast with us. Guns were heard in the distance, and the " Union Jack " was seen flying from Allumbagh, which all seem to think means that Sir Colin Campbell has reached that place with his force. Mr. Kavanagh, the head clerk in Mr. Cooper's office, volunteered to go out last night to Allumbagh, and conduct our force into Lucknow. It was a most gallant act, and all were delighted when the signal agreed upon to announce his arrival (the hoisting a flag) was spied from the top of the Residency about twelve o'clock this morning. Mr. Kavanagh went out about eight o'clock disguised as a native, with a man with him as a guide. Captain Dodgson, assistant-adjutant-general to the force here, called on us to-day. He is related to or connected with our dear friends the Scotts of Brotherton. We are so grieved to hear that there is every chance of poor Colonel Campbell being obliged to have his leg amputated. He is not so well to-day, and when Colonel Inglis went to see him he was wandering a good deal. I scarcely know why, but this has been to me a wretched day; some days one feels more especially depressed, and to me this has been one of them.

Wednesday, November 11th.

No messenger has been in to-day, and I have heard no news of any kind. Poor Colonel Campbell had his leg amputated to-day. Fortunately they were able to get some chloroform from Dr. Fayrer. We hear that so far he is doing well, but he is very weak, and I fear that there is much danger of his not getting over it. We have had a visit from Mr. Harmer. His leg is getting much better and he is now able to put on a slipper and can put his foot to the ground. In the afternoon we arranged some of our things, separating those we were anxious to keep, and those we wished to part with. Mrs. Roberts came for some work to do for me, and Mrs. Campbell came and finally arranged to go to England with Mrs. Inglis. She brought home some little warm jackets she had made for the children.

Thursday, November 12th.

THE telegraph, which works from the top of the Residency, and is replied to by the one from Allumbagh, announces that Sir Colin Campbell has arrived there. He is to advance with his force on Lucknow to-morrow, and is expected to arrive here on Sunday. They are to come in by the Dil Khoosha. Most fervently is it to be hoped that their entrance into Lucknow may be successful, and that this time we really may be released from our captivity. The enemy made an attack on Allumbagh this morning, but our troops got possession of two of their guns.

There will be some more hard fighting before they get in.

Colonel Campbell is so weak and ill that he is not expected to live till the morning. He is quite insensible, but does not appear to suffer much. Captain Barrow and Captain Dodgson came to see us this evening. We did not dine till very late. I hear that an attack is expected to-night; they are certainly firing a good deal, but as yet (ten P.M.) nothing like an attack has commenced.

Friday, November 13th.

SHARP musketry was heard in the direction of Allumbagh this morning. The telegraph has been at work, and from it we learn that Sir Colin Campbell is to march to-morrow morning at seven. An important letter from him to Sir James Outram has been lost; but another has been written, which may come in to-night. The insurgents appear to be increasing in numbers round this place. The rebels who have escaped from Delhi have come here, and are, it is said, holding the outposts. They still seem to think that there will be an attack made upon us, and all are in readiness to meet it. Colonel Inglis told us to-day, that since General Havelock's force came in (October 25th), 100 of his own garrison had been killed and wounded, and twenty-six of the 32nd killed. Captain Barrow dined with us. Poor Colonel Campbell died last night about eleven o'clock. Mrs. Giddings came to see us this evening; and told us it is reported that the enemy wanted Captain Orr (their prisoner) to show them how to make shells and the way to take the Baillie Gate. Gave the servants some warm clothes to-day.

Saturday, November 14th.

VERY heavy firing was heard this morning between twelve and one; and our flag was seen flying from the Martinière College. Sir Colin's force has got possession of the Dil Khoosha Palace; and we are told that the officers were seen through a telescope smoking their cigars on the top of the house. To-morrow will be a most anxious day, as they will have to come through the city. A sortie is to be made by some of the troops in garrison in the morning, in order to take the Kaiser Bagh Palace, and so divert the attention of the rebels. All must feel most deeply for the poor prisoners whose fate is in the hands of these wretches; but as we have prisoners also, it is to be hoped this may be a check on any bad intentions which may be entertained by the insurgents. Mrs. Giddings came to see us and told us that poor Mrs. Ouseley died this morning, which shocked us much, as we had not even heard that she was ill. She was only laid up for a few days with dysentery and fever, and sank, from complete exhaustion. It is sad to think of all the distress poor Colonel Palmer has gone through during this siege; and now his little boy is so ill, that it is doubtful whether he will recover. Mrs. Roberts came this evening with some things she has been making for us; and told us she had sat up all last night with poor Mrs. Ouseley. I went to see Mrs. Radclyffe and as usual found Mrs. Clarke with her. She's a kind little creature. This has been a very quiet day. No firing till towards evening.

Sunday, November 15th.

SIR COLIN's force did not advance yesterday as was expected, but remained stationary at the Dil Khoosha, and a great deal of excitement pervaded our garrison, all being on the look-out to watch the movements of his troops. The day has been very quiet, with the exception of a gun of the enemy's occasionally firing near Major Banks's house. Attended Divine Service. This is Colonel Inglis's birthday; Captain Barrow dined with us, and gave us an account of the wonderful escape he, his wife, and family had, in getting away from Salone, where he was commissioner, just in time to save their lives; and, strange to say, the very man who saved them is now fighting against us; the account of his adventures interested us very much.

The extraordinary infatuation of officers in native corps never choosing to believe it possible that their regiments could prove faithless, is one of the most remarkable features in the whole of this mutiny. Every thing is said to be quiet at Delhi and Agra, but it is strange that a regiment (the 50th I believe) has mutinied after every thing had settled down there, and after they had been held up as patterns of fidelity and loyalty. We had a fruit-pie for dinner to-day, a thing we have not had for four months, and the poor children enjoyed it greatly.

Monday, November 16*th.*

LAST night, about ten o'clock, the enemy began to fire heavily. It did not last very long; but was again commenced and was very loud indeed about four o'clock in the morning, after which it gradually subsided. Distant guns were heard, and we fear that there must have been some fighting during the night. We have had a very anxious day, and much firing has been heard during the whole morning, and till about three o'clock P.M., when it ceased. Sir Colin's force has now advanced some distance on this side of our old bungalows, and will not get here till to-morrow. They have come only a short way to-day, but that is all the better, and they seem to be getting on well so far, though it is impossible to say whether there has been much loss of life on our side. A party was sent out from the garrison this morning to take some houses, three were killed, and twenty-one wounded: too many for what they accomplished. This will be a most anxious night. The garrison is, I believe, to be reinforced, and every thing made ready to repulse an attack, should there be one. Captain Birch has had a most narrow escape. A bullet just grazed his ear and entered his hat. Fortunately it is a mere scratch; but this is the second time since the commencement of the siege that he has been hit.

Tuesday, November 17th.

WE were much surprised that last night passed off so quietly; indeed scarcely any firing was heard. Sir Colin's force was seen to advance very slowly, that is to say, artillery only were visible, *no infantry.* About two o'clock we heard that " red jackets " were in the 32nd Mess-house, and soon after that they had possession of Mr. Martin's house. About four o'clock, a sight we had not seen for a very long time caught our eyes; two officers, each leading a horse and coming into our court-yard inquiring for Colonel Inglis. We at once saw that they belonged to the advancing force, and we were told that one of them was Colonel Berkeley, the new Colonel of the 32nd. Just before dinner, Colonel Inglis brought him up and introduced him to us.

Colonel Napier has been wounded to-day in the leg, but not dangerously I believe and hope, for so useful an officer can be ill dispensed with now.

When Colonel Inglis came to dinner he told us that Sir Colin Campbell's orders are that we are all to leave Lucknow to-morrow evening! Our consternation may be more easily imagined than described, and I think our faces when we looked at each other wore an expression of the most complete bewilderment. How all the wounded and sick people and women and children are to be got off in such a hurried manner, at only a few hours' notice, I cannot imagine.

Wednesday, November 18*th.*

It was found impracticable to get the women
and children off to-day, so only the sick and
wounded were sent, and we were told that
we should not have to move till to-morrow.
We were busy packing up the whole day and
trying to compress our few things in as small
a space as possible, not knowing for how
much we should be allowed carriage. Our
linen we sewed up in pillow-cases and took
as pillows; the other things which we ab-
solutely did not want to leave behind us
we put into boxes. We contrived to take a
good deal of our plate among our clothes,
but all our glass and crockery we were
obliged to leave behind us, besides many
other things we should like to have saved.
We had some visitors in the evening, and I

went over to see Mrs. Cooper and Mrs. Radclyffe. We went to our beds very late, for we could not help talking over our strange situation and the probable events of the following day.

Evacuation

CHAP. XIII.

Thursday, November 19th.

WE were up early this morning to finish all we had to do, and were several times interrupted by visitors ; General Grant, Colonel Berkeley, and Captain Lowe were among them. Several of the ladies left the Residency as early as ten o'clock, and people were going out the whole day long. Colonel Inglis thought it better that we should start later, and it was arranged that four P.M. should be the hour. We got some Coolies to carry our charpoys, and procured a hackery for our boxes. They all preceded us by a couple of hours. We had some soup before starting, and were, I believe, about the last to leave the Residency. Strange indeed were our feelings on leaving

our courtyard and that confined space
where we had spent so many wretched hours.
Mr. Birch (A.D.C.) was sent by Colonel
Inglis to escort us as far as Secundra Bagh,
as he could not go with us himself; we knew
not if we should remain there the night or
go on to the Dil Khoosha. We three ladies
and Captain Birch started on foot, and the
children and ayah in our shattered little carriage drawn by Coolies. Had we not known
that it really was our carriage, we scarcely
could have believed what a wreck it had become. A round shot had gone through the
head, it was pierced with bullets, and in fact it
was tattered to pieces; a wretched horse which
could hardly walk was the only thing to be
found to draw the buggy which followed
empty.

The scene of ruin, devastation, and misery
which presented itself to our eyes when we
got out I *never, never* shall forget. To de-

scribe it would be impossible; but the horrors of war presented themselves with full force in the mass of shattered buildings and dilapidated gateways through which we passed. Three short bits of road were dangerous, as the enemy could, from the top of a mosque, see people going along, and fire on them. At these places we had to take the children out of the carriage, and have them carried,—and all our party ran as fast as we could. I am thankful to say that we arrived safely at Secundra Bagh, about half-past five o'clock. Mrs. Inglis and Caroline walked the whole way; I, the greater part.

The scene at Secundra is a most strange one; it is a garden enclosed within high walls. On Tuesday last Sir Colin's troops had an engagement with the enemy, and killed, some say 2000, others 1500, of them in this very place: they were all buried yesterday. Here were now assembled all the ladies, women, and children who had left the Residency. We had our charpoys carried inside, and seated ourselves upon them. The officers were going about, most kindly bringing wine and biscuits to those who wished to take any thing ; and numbers were busily employed in arranging about the conveyances to take us all on to the Dil Khoosha, whither, we were told, we were to proceed in two or three hours. Many kindly inquired whether we had all we required, and Sir Colin amongst them. Major Ouvry, of the 9th Lancers, offered us a bullock gharry of his own to go in, of which we gladly availed ourselves, and we three, and the three children, with another lady and child, all got in, and, as Mrs. Inglis said, were packed as closely as a box of sardines.

We had an escort of 1500 men to go with our column, which was a very long one. We were ordered to proceed very quietly, and silence was constantly enforced, so that the enemy's attention might not be attracted towards us. We had proceeded some distance, when the column came to a halt; and we imagine that the advanced guard must have heard some noise which caused alarm, for they sent back to Secundra Bagh for a reinforcement.

We reached the Dil Khoosha about midnight, and among all the camels, waggons, Coolies, and people moving in every direction, it was difficult to know where the tent was situated to which we were to proceed; but Colonel Little, the Brigadier, to whom Mrs. Inglis had brought a note, came to our rescue, and took us to a large tent where there were a great many other ladies. It was not enclosed, but we were only too glad of shelter of any kind; and Azaib soon put up the beds. Colonel Little, and several other officers of the 9th Lancers, kindly brought us tea, bread and butter, and pudding, which we enjoyed very much,—four months having elapsed since we had seen anything of the kind. By the time we had made ourselves comfortable for the night (lying down under the rezais, without undressing), it must have been two o'clock. However, tired as I was, I slept well for two or three hours. I was the first awake, and I could not help thinking, as I lay there and looked around me, what a strange position we poor unfortunate creatures were all placed in. But we might have been in a worse condition ; and the longest life will not be sufficient to pour forth our gratitude for our merciful preservation through all the dangers of the siege.

Friday, November 20th.

WE got the large tent, which Colonel Inglis brought from Dr. Fayrer, pitched early this morning, and were delighted to change our quarters, and be able to wash and dress comfortably.   There is a nice division in it, and as we had plenty of room in one half, Mrs. Inglis most kindly gave the other to Mrs. and Miss Birch, the former being an invalid.   Very grateful they were to be allowed to share a tent so much more comfortable than the one they had been in during the night.   After we were dressed, we went over to breakfast with the 9th Lancers.   The table was laid out under the trees, and the whole thing looked very cool and pleasant. We enjoyed the bread and butter and jam, and a cup of coffee very much, for they were things we had not tasted for a long time. Our chief occupation during the day was arranging our things, and Mrs. Inglis had a great many visitors.   I did not go out this evening ; Mrs. Inglis and Carry strolled about the camp.

Letters recieved from England first contact 4 months

Saturday, November 21st.

To-day we all got a great many English letters, and very sad they were to receive. The anxiety in England is heartrending to think of, and public sympathy seems indeed to be bestowed upon us to the very highest degree. The latest dates of our letters were 11th September. Captain Edgehill, who seems to have the management of the carriage required by the ladies, has been constantly during the day with a pen and paper at our door. We find that each lady is allowed a camel and a cart. I am sure even the few things that we have, and all the servants' bundles and pillows stuffed with their property (most of which they looted in the Residency), cannot possibly be taken if we do not get more carriage for them. No

order yet about our move, but we should not
take long to be ready. No one seems to
know when we shall march. I suppose they
do not wish the natives to know anything
about our movements. In the evening Carry
and I strolled about, and walked some time
with Mrs. Brydon and Mrs. Clarke. The
ladies all seem very comfortable. Heard to-
day that Dr. Derby and young Mr. Dashwood were dead; both, no doubt, having
been the worse for the move. We dined late
outside our tent.

Sunday, November 22nd.

WHILE we were dressing this morning the
enemy made an attack. The musketry
did not last very long. The 9th Lancers
went out, but soon returned. They killed
some of the enemy in a village, and among

others a metah, at which our servants were
very indignant. The rest of the day was
very quiet. Still no order to move. We
are very anxious to-night, knowing that the
whole force was to leave the Residency to-day.
They began to move out about one o'clock
P.M. Colonel Inglis, who was with the
rear-guard, did not leave till midnight. We
heard a good deal of musketry during the
night, which gave us some alarm ; but it
turned out to be the enemy firing on the Residency after the whole force had left. However, all our people arrived at the Dil Khoosha
quite safely, without having seen one of the
insurgents.

One officer (Captain Waterman, of the
13th Native Infantry) was very near being
left behind. He had fallen asleep, and awoke
up suddenly much surprised to find every
thing so quiet all round him. He jumped
up, found every one gone, and ran as hard as

he could till he overtook the force some little way beyond the Residency. It would have been far from a pleasant fate to have been left alone to the mercy of those whom he knew would rush in as soon as they found we were gone. Musketry was still heard when we went to bed, and Colonel Inglis had not arrived at eleven o'clock. Mrs. Inglis did not undress, in order that she might be ready to get up at any moment.

Monday, November 23rd.

COLONEL INGLIS arrived this morning about six, having been out all night, and all are now safe at the Dil Khoosha.

Wednesday, November 25th.

ALL was confusion and bustle this morning.
To know what a camp such as ours is when
getting ready for a start, it must be seen.
The hackeries, camels, elephants, vehicles of
all sorts, servants rushing about, every one
looking after their boxes and baggage, presented a most extraordinary scene. We were
up very early, being told that we should
march at eleven o'clock. When we had
settled our things we sat down to some tea
and bread and butter, having decided that
we would not make a regular breakfast.
Mrs. Giddings came and staid for a long
time. Not being able to get bullocks for the
carriage and buggy, we got a native hackery.
Mrs. Inglis, Carry, myself, and baby went
into it ; Johnny, Charlie, and the ayah

stretcher to carry one person

going in a doolie. It was some time before
we got fairly off, for we were very much in
the rear, and found ourselves among the baggage and camels. The dust was something
fearful, and at times the heat very great.
We get on slowly, having constant stoppages.
We did not reach our encampment, which
is about a mile from Allumbagh, till nearly
six o'clock; so that it took us nearly six
hours from the time we started till we were
on the spot where our tent was to be pitched.
The hackeries, with our things, and every
thing on which we had depended for dinner,
were anxiously looked for for a long time,
without making their appearance. Being so
late we had the small tent belonging to Colonel Inglis pitched instead of our large one.

I do not know what we should have done
had it not been for the great kindness of
General Grant, 9th Lancers, who himself
brought us a bottle of beer, some tongue,

and some excellent bread and butter; and not satisfied with *that*, returned a second time, bringing us some tea. We were very tired, and as soon as we had finished our repast we lay down on the ground in the tent, and rolled ourselves up in the blankets and rezais, and slept soundly, hard as was our bed. Just as we were starting this morning we heard of the death of poor General Havelock: this is a hard fate, just as he had so well earned all his honours!

Thursday, November 26th.

FINDING we were to remain at Allumbagh we had the large tent pitched. Sir James Outram and all his force arrived here to-day. Captain Barrow came to see us as soon as he arrived. We have our large tent all to ourselves, so we enjoyed the luxury of a bath, and spent so much time over it, that it was very late when we breakfasted. Colonel Inglis was with us. We strolled out a short distance, but did not see any one. Colonel Inglis dined with us.

Friday, November 27th.

I FELT so unwell that Mrs. Inglis and Caroline insisted on my remaining the greater part of the day in bed, as we had a prospect of so much fatigue before us. I got up about four o'clock in the afternoon. Colonel Inglis dined with us. As we were told we should march at seven to-morrow morning we only took off our dresses and laid down on our beds.

Saturday, November 28th.

GOT up very early and prepared all for a start at seven, but just as we were dressed, Captain Edgehill came and told us that we should not go till eleven o'clock. We are very well off for conveyances, Captain Probyn having lent Mrs. Inglis his bullock gharry, and Mr. Jackson insisted on our taking his carriage with a couple of mules. The children and the ayah go in the bullock gharry, and ourselves and baby in the carriage. We started about half-past ten o'clock, and had a most tedious day's march. I think we were one hour and a half sitting in the carriages without moving. To imagine the sight of so many hackeries, camels, carriages of all kinds, riders, camp-followers, &c., is quite impossible without having been an eye-witness of the scene. And how they are ever brought into any degree of order, and how all arrive at their destination, appears a perfect wonder. The whole column was nine miles in length. The name of the place where we are encamped to-night I do not know, but it is about nine miles from Allumbagh. Even getting over that short distance took us more than seven hours, as it was nearly six o'clock when we reached the spot where our tent was to be pitched. Captain Rudman was very kind in assisting us to get the tent up and to collect our things. We made him remain and have some dinner with us, but we were so tired that we were glad when the dinner was over, and we could once more lie down on the ground and go to sleep. Mrs. Inglis was fairly knocked up. I do not think I ever saw her look more so.

Sunday, November 29th.

WE started at seven this morning, and I think, if possible, it has been a more tedious day than yesterday. The march was very long, and the train proceeded very slowly.   We halted in the course of the day for about an hour, when Mrs. Inglis was able to get some arrow-root made on the roadside for poor baby, and we had fortunately taken some milk with us, and bread and butter for the other children. We passed Mhow and came to a place within three miles of the river.   We did not reach our ground till ten, all fairly tired out. We must have marched nearly thirty miles to-day.   A great deal of firing was heard at Cawnpore.   No one appeared to know what it was, but it was evident that fighting was

fighting at Cawnpore

going on.   Another night again without being able to undress, but nevertheless we all sleep soundly.

Monday, November 30th.

WE started this morning later than usual; we were, however, up early waiting for orders, but as none arrived, we thought it better to have breakfast.   Colonel Inglis came and had some tea with us, but he was in such a hurry that he had not time to take any thing more. We saw fires at Cawnpore, evidently stores or bungalows being burned.   We heard that there had been some fighting there yesterday, when Brigadier Wilson and several of the 64th were killed.   I was very sorry to hear of the death of the former, he had always been a kind friend to me, and I know how much his family will regret him.   Our troops went out to meet the enemy, I believe, under the orders of General Wyndham, and we were but 1500 against 20,000. We hear various reports, but it appears certain that the Gwalior Force is attacking Cawnpore, and that is the reason, no doubt, that they are hurrying us on. It really seems as if we never should get out of our difficulties; fighting seems to follow in our train, or rather, I should say, to precede us wherever we go.

After we had finished breakfast, Captain Edgehill came and told us we ought to be ready to start at ten o'clock. We had only one mile and a half to go; but that short distance took us an hour. We pitched our small tent as soon as we could, and the air being delicious, we sat out and read for some time; and then Colonel Inglis and Colonel Shortt came up. When they went away we read the evening service, but how little it appeared like a quiet holy Sunday, all around us speaking of war and its attendant horrors.

At four P.M. we dined; Colonel Inglis and Captain Wilson shared our dinner, and Captain Birch, who arrived just as we had finished our soup, was very glad to sit on a box outside and partake of what we had; something to eat in these times, and especially a glass of beer, being most acceptable, and not always procurable. We were told that about seven P.M. we should be ready to start, so the small tent was soon struck, and we were once more *en route* for Cawnpore. When we got upon the road, we found the mass of hackeries, camels, and vehicles worse than ever,—four lines deep on the road. However, most fortunately, General Grant had ordered part of the road to be cleared for the carriages, so we got on very well with the exception of a few long stoppages and some heavy parts through the sand. When we arrived at last at the bridge, some very sharp musketry was heard close to us. I must say I felt alarmed, thinking that the party in front was being attacked, but it turned out to be our own people firing at what they thought were some of the enemy ; but I believe it was a false alarm.

11 days to get to Cawnpore

At last we arrived at Cawnpore, and nothing could look more wretched and miserable than this dreadful place as we came in by the light of the moon. The burnt bungalows, the broken gates, the remains of gun carriages, trees lying on the ground with their leaves and branches completely stripped off, and more than all, the thoughts which arose in our minds of the fearful scenes so lately enacted here depressed and saddened us altogther. It was now twelve o'clock at night, and we were brought to the Dragoon Barracks. Our small tent was up as soon as ourselves, and pitched in a few minutes. We had some hot tea, and once again the ground in our tent formed our only bed, and we did not dream of undressing.

they were no massacre

fear

Monday, November 30th.

WE were so uncertain as to what would be our orders for to-day, that we waited till ten o'clock; and nothing being heard, we each took it by turns to bathe and dress in the tent, and it was past one before we were all ready for breakfast.   We were then told that we were to be moved at once to the Artillery Barracks, but we quietly ate our breakfast, thinking that probably another order would shortly be issued, and so it turned out to be; for we are now told to hold ourselves in readiness for a start at daylight to-morrow. Captain Norman came just before we sat down to dinner, and talked a little of the affairs of the country.   He seems to think that it will be rather a long business putting every thing to rights again.   There is one place still in a state of siege in Central India, called Saugor, and *that* of course a force must go to relieve. It is a small garrison, I think Captain Norman said 220 men and 170 women and children; but they are said to be able to hold out for some time. Captain Wilson amused us the other day by telling us that when our force came away from the Residency, they left 30,000 rupees (three thousand pounds) in pice. It appears almost an incredible thing that such a large sum could have been collected in that way. Of course the great weight prevented its being moved. No doubt the natives had a good scramble for it.

pice — dd बी subunit of currency.
— four work an anna

anna — one-sixteenth of rupee

CHAP. XIV.

Tuesday, December 1st.

AT seven o'clock this morning every one in camp was on the move, and various groups were taking their chotah hazree outside their tents; camels were being loaded, and all the carriages were ready by half-past seven o'clock. It was very cold indeed when we started. Our move was to the Artillery Barracks, which is a great improvement on our position of the morning. It took us about half an hour to get here, and we found a very nice piece of encamping ground. We pitched the large tent at once, and made ourselves very comfortable. Poor Brigadier Wilson's old servant, Saville, came to see me to-day, to ask me to write to Mrs. Wilson, which I intend to do, painful as the task will be. The poor man appeared so dreadfully grieved, that I was quite sorry to see him. The last moments of the Brigadier appear to have been tranquil. He spent in prayer the half hour that he lived after he was taken into his tent.

It is fortunate that we left the Dragoon Barracks when we did, for during the day an officer, a man, and a boy, were wounded, and a camel, pony, and an elephant, were killed, by " shrapnel " from the insurgents. No one knows any thing about our movements, but all seem to say that we cannot leave Cawnpore till things are quieter.

Wednesday, December 2nd.

LAST night we all undressed and had a very good night, going really to bed. We were told, early in the morning, that we should march in the course of the day, and repeatedly had the fact impressed upon us that we must be ready to start at half-an-hour's notice. Captain Edgehill came and begged us to send, at twelve o'clock, for eight days' rations, which we did; but another order was then issued, that four o'clock was to be the hour. We were kept in this suspense all day, and towards evening were told that we should not go till night, and perhaps not till daybreak. At half-past four o'clock, Carry and I walked with Mr. and Mrs. Harris to see the place where all the poor people who were murdered here maintained so fierce a struggle with the fiends outside. I could not have believed, had I not seen it, that their abode had been so wretched. They were shut up here for twenty-one days. The intrenchment is scarcely even a good-sized ditch, and yet, at times, it was safer for the poor ladies to take their chairs and sit there than to remain in the miserable building which scarcely afforded a shelter from the sun. The roof had been entirely destroyed by round shot, and the only thing which showed there had once been a verandah were a few solitary beams of wood projecting from the main building.

It was sad to see pieces of old letters, parts of old returns of the dear old 32nd, and here and there a sheet of torn music, strewn about the ground. Mrs. Harris picked up part of an old Bible. As to a door or a window, not a vestige of such a thing remains ; and the wretched attempt at a gate, in order to form a barricade, which the garrison had erected, showed to what extremities the poor sufferers must have been reduced. We saw the only well from which they could get water, and it was under such a heavy fire, that they had to run out when it was dark and draw the water as they could. The enemy were in houses *close* to them, and in great numbers, and yet never had the courage to come over the miserable intrenchment. In some places there were scraps of writing on the wall, describing their sufferings. In one place Caroline found the following words, " Dear Jesus, send us help to-day, and deliver us not into the hands of our enemies ! " Poor things, how excruciating must have been their agony. No doubt to many, the holy faith of Jesus, — the confidence they felt in our Heavenly Father, was a support which made them peaceful and happy even in their greatest extremity.

When one sees the place where these poor creatures were shut up, the wonder is that any one ever lived to get out of it. Very many indeed died, and the only place in which they had to bury them was a well, into which the bodies were thrown at night!!! But still, I believe, nearly 400 got out alive, and were reserved for a much more cruel fate. The place where they were afterwards murdered, by order of the brutal Nana, is now in possession of the enemy, so of course we did not attempt to see it.

Colonel Inglis dined with us. Captain Rudman came in the evening. He looks very ill, and I do not think he will be able to stand this kind of life long. The management of the troops here in the action the other day seems to have been very bad, and severe comments are made on the officer in command. We little expected to find Cawnpore in such a state. The insurgents are all round it, and are in possession of the city. I dare say the Commander-in-Chief hardly knows what to do with us. Most anxious he is, no doubt, to get us away; but after escaping the dangers of the Lucknow siege, I am sure he would not like to expose us to more danger than is necessary. We sent off our English letters to-day, and I wrote to poor Mrs. Wilson, at Deesa, telling her of the death of her husband. As we thought we should not have more than half an hour's notice to start, we did not undress, but lay down as we were. I cannot say I slept very well, and the want of a proper night's rest knocks me up more than any thing else. I feel very tired and good for nothing to-day. Heard that a man of the 88th was taken prisoner yesterday.

Thursday, December 3rd.

WE have been expecting, since the early morning, to get our orders to move every moment. It is now past four o'clock and we have heard nothing about it; so we are still in a state of uncertainty which is most unpleasant. We went again this afternoon to the old intrenchments with Mrs. Inglis, who had not been with us the day before. As we were returning we met Colonel Inglis, and he said he did not think it likely that we should go this evening; but, however, as soon as we got back to our tent we found that Captain Edgehill had been to say the order had come for us to march at ten o'clock to-night, so we ordered our dinner at once, and sent up to tell Colonel

Inglis we were now really going; prepared as we had been all day for our start. There always remain a few things which can only be done just at the last. About half-past nine o'clock Colonel Inglis came to our tent, with Captain Birch, who came to say good-bye. Every thing appeared very sad and gloomy starting at that hour of the night, and to poor Mrs. Inglis the parting from her husband at such a time and in such a manner was very distressing. I felt very much for her. He walked down with us to the place where our gharry started from, and there we all parted. It was miserable work; and I had such a severe cold and felt so ill, that I was in a bad condition to commence so fatiguing a journey. Our escort consists of the 34th Regiment, some cavalry, and four guns.

Friday, December 4th.

OUR journey last night was tedious. Though we started at ten o'clock, we did not reach our encamping ground till eleven this morning. We marched twenty-seven miles, and were all dreadfully tired. I do not know that in my whole life I ever felt more so, for we had been able to get very little sleep during the night. The children's gharry most unfortunately broke down, the wheel coming off; so we were obliged to move the children and all the boxes into our carriage, which delayed us, and made us fall a good deal to the rear. Mrs. Inglis wrote a few lines to Colonel Inglis, and gave her note to one of the officers we met on the road marching up to Cawnpore with different detachments of regiments, of which there appeared to be a good many. Our tent is pitched in a nice grove of trees; Mrs. Gall and her party are our nearest neighbours. A very sad accident happened last night. A writer's wife, whose husband was shot during the siege, is travelling with her brother. They were in a buggy; he got out and left his rifle against the door of the carriage, which moved on, and the poor woman, thinking the gun would fall to the ground, put her hand on the muzzle of it to prevent its doing so. It went off and shot her hand, shattering it so much that as soon as we arrived on the encamping ground she was obliged to have her thumb amputated, and it seems doubtful whether she will not lose her hand. She was close to us, and it was painful to think of her sufferings, she seemed to be so patient. She could only travel on a charpoy, and there was much difficulty in procuring Coolies; but Mrs.

Inglis, with her usual kindness, gave her two of hers, and she was able to get four herself. We dined at five, and afterwards I was so tired that I lay down and fell asleep for about an hour, just before they struck the tent.

Saturday, December 5th.

WE got off last night about ten, and arrived on our ground this morning at seven, having marched only twelve miles, so we came along very slowly indeed; and I believe we halted for two hours during the night, but we all slept, and none of our party knew it. We are encamped in a nice place to-day, and are near a pretty piece of water. Mrs. Giddings breakfasted with us; she is quite alone, and Mrs. Inglis has asked her to come and breakfast and dine with us always, as she has no servants of her own. We are eight miles from Futtypore, and shall pass it to-night.

Sunday, December 6th.

THE march was weary, long, and tedious (sixteen miles), with constant delays, and we were so tired and cramped up in the palkie gharry, that I do not know how we shall ever get through another night in it. We reached our encamping ground about seven A. M., and the morning was cold and chilly. Neither the camels nor the servants belonging to the kitchen department had made their appearance when we arrived; the former, however, soon came up, and our tent was pitched under a pretty grove of trees. We waited some time for the khansamah and kitmaghars, and finding they did not arrive,

we got out all the breakfast things, and laid
the table; fortunately, we had the remains
of a cold fowl with us, and one of the other
servants made the chupatties. Just as we had
seated ourselves at breakfast the khansamah
arrived. They had all fallen asleep, at some
place where they lay down to rest, and did not
awake till a very late hour, causing a long
delay, which for us was rather inconvenient.
After breakfast it was very late (two o'clock,
I believe), and we read the Evening Service.
I lay down in the tent for about an hour, but
got up more tired, I think. Carry and I
walked through the camp, and saw Mrs. and
Miss Halford. We are to start again at
nine to-night.

Monday, December 7th.

ANOTHER night more fatiguing than ever; we arrived at the railroad at six A.M., and were told that we should have to get into the train at once. To describe the scene of confusion with all the hackeries, camels, and conveyances of every kind, would be impossible. No one seemed to know what they were to do with their luggage. Some people said it could not go with us, others that it could. We got out of our own conveyance and took possession of one of the railway carriages, putting in all our small parcels and boxes with us. It was soon made known that the luggage *could* go with us, so we had the camels unloaded, and their loads transferred to the luggage-vans, also some things out of the hackery ; but we found it much better to let the latter and the goats follow us. The gharrywarr said they would be up on Wednesday morning. There were great delays in the starting of the train, and we did not finally get off till ten o'clock, which was annoying, as the time spent in sitting in the railroad-carriage might have been employed in getting a comfortable breakfast; instead of which, we got nothing to eat till our arrival at Allahabad, which we reached between two and three o'clock. The distance we came by rail was, I believe, about forty miles. Nothing could exceed the warm and enthusiastic welcome with which we were received at Allahabad. All the soldiers cheered as we arrived, and every kind of conveyance, doolies, buggies, and carriages, were in readiness to take us to the tents which, by the Governor-General's order, were pitched for us. Mrs. Inglis, the three children, and innumerable small but heavy boxes, were put into a dooly; but the bearers had not gone many yards, before they declared their inability to go farther, the weight being too great. A gentleman, who fortunately happened to be passing in a carriage at the time, made Mrs. Inglis get in, and drove her up to the tent. Mrs. Giddings came in a dooly, and, lastly, Carry and I had to be provided, for I was suffering greatly from a swollen ankle, and was altogether so tired and knocked up that I could scarcely move a step. I was therefore looking out most anxiously for some assistance, when Dr. Scott came and told us that there was a gentleman here with a dog-cart, who would drive us up. We lost no time in getting in, and picked up Mrs. Thomson on the road, who was walking, and looking dreadfully tired. Nothing can be more perfect than all the arrangements made here by the authorities for the ladies. The tents, which are very large ones, are pitched in a pretty spot, and the whole encamping ground is shut in with kanauts, so that we are perfectly private. I felt so very unwell that I really scarcely knew what was going on around me. We did not get any dinner till nearly seven o'clock; and though I had scarcely tasted any thing since the previous day, I felt very little inclined to eat, and was only too glad to undress and go to my bed as soon as it was ready. Nothing could exceed the attention and kindness of those who had provided for our comfort here. Lights and soap were taken round to every tent, with sago for the children, as well as milk.

Tuesday, December 8th.

IT was indeed a great relief to undress again, it being the first time for five nights : all that time we had never taken off our clothes, except to change them. I was so completely tired, that when I went to bed I got into such a high state of fever I could not sleep, and got no rest till towards the early morning, and I was soon so unwell that we were obliged to send for Dr. Scott. He seemed to think it was only fatigue, and said that I required strengthening ; and he would send me some quinine. I remained in bed the whole day, almost unconscious of what was going on ; but heard enough to know that they were all busy with bon and copra-wallahs the greater part of the day.

Monday, December 14th.

THE last five days I have been so ill I could
not continue my journal. I felt better yesterday; but to-day do not feel so well.
The weather is very chilly; perhaps that is
one of the reasons. But I trust it may
please God to bless the means used for my
recovery, and spare me to see you all again.

APPENDIX.

In the chancel of St. Chad's Church, a memorial
has been erected to the late Rev. H. S. Polehampton.
The inscription, from the pen of the Rev. B. H.
Kennedy, D.D., is as follows: —

" Sacred to the memory of the REVEREND HENRY
STEDMAN POLEHAMPTON, M.A., late Fellow of Pem-
broke College, Oxford, and nearly seven years curate
of this parish. Appointed a Chaplain of the Hon.
East India Company, and stationed at Lucknow. He
was one of the small garrison who valiantly defended
the British Residency against a vast besieging force
of native insurgents; and amidst his sacred functions
was wounded by a bullet through his body, and died
twelve days later of cholera, July 20th, 1857, aged
33 years. Endowed with sound abilities, a kind heart,
and liberal mind; uniting energy with simplicity, and
tempering zeal with moderation, he received testi-
monies of grateful esteem from those to whom he
ministered both in England and in India; and as he
had comforted many sufferers, so in his own hour of
suffering he derived full comfort from the great Scrip-
tural promise of salvation through faith in Christ
Jesus.

" His wife Emily, youngest daughter of Charles
Blake Allnatt, Esq., having shared his perils and

watched his death-bed, was, with the other surviving Europeans, providentially rescued by British troops under British commanders, whose matchless feats of devoted courage will live in history and in the hearts of their countrymen.

"This tablet was erected by private subscription, in remembrance of a beloved friend and pastor."

The memorial is entirely of Carrara marble, of chaste and elegant design. Over the cornice is an unfolded book, upon the leaves of which are inscribed the words, "Enter thou into the joy of thy Lord." Behind this is the cross, and branches of the Eastern palm. The tablet is placed in the chancel, near to that of his grandfather, the late Rev. Thomas Stedman.

The following narrative of the defence of Lucknow by Brigadier Inglis supplies those interesting military details which cannot be looked for in a lady's journal:—

BRIGADIER INGLIS'S NARRATIVE OF THE DEFENCE OF LUCKNOW.

"*From Brigadier Inglis, commanding Garrison of Lucknow, to the Secretary to Government, Military Department, Calcutta.*

"Dated Lucknow, Sept. 26.

"Sir,—In consequence of the very deeply-to-be-lamented death of Brigadier-General Sir H. M. Lawrence, K.C.B., late in command of the Oude Field Force, the duty of narrating the military events which

have occurred at Lucknow since the 29th of June last
has devolved upon myself.

"On the evening of that day reports reached
Sir Henry Lawrence that the rebel army, in no very
inconsiderable force, would march from Chinhut (a
small village about eight miles distant on the road to
Fyzabad) on Lucknow on the following morning; and
the late Brigadier-General therefore determined to
make a strong reconnoissance in that direction, with
the view, if possible, of meeting the force at a dis-
advantage, either at its entrance into the suburbs of
the city, or at the bridge across the Gokral, which is
a small stream intersecting the Fyzabad road, about
half-way between Lucknow and Chinhut.

"The force destined for this service, and which
was composed as follows, moved out at six A. M. on the
morning of the 30th of June:—Artillery: four guns of
No. — Horse Light Field Battery, four ditto of No. 2
Oude Field Battery, two ditto of No. 3 ditto ditto,
and an 8-inch howitzer. Cavalry: Troop of Volunteer Cavalry; 120 troopers of detachments belonging
to 1st, 2nd, and 3rd Regiments of Oude Irregular
Cavalry. Infantry: 300, Her Majesty's 32nd; 150,
13th Native Infantry; 60, 48th Native Infantry; 20,
71st Native Infantry (Sikhs).

"The troops, misled by the reports of wayfarers—
who stated that there were few or no men between
Lucknow and Chinhut—proceeded somewhat further
than had been originally intended, and suddenly fell
in with the enemy, who had up to that time eluded
the vigilance of the advanced guard by concealing
themselves behind a long line of trees in overwhelming
numbers. The European force and howitzer, with
the Native Infantry, held the foe in check for some

time, and had six guns of the Oude artillery been faithful and the Sikh Cavalry shown a better front, the day would have been won in spite of an immense disparity in numbers. But the Oude artillerymen and drivers were traitors. They overturned the guns into the ditches, cut the traces of their horses, and abandoned them, regardless of the remonstrances and exertions of their own officers, and of those of Sir Henry Lawrence's staff, headed by the Brigadier-General in person, who himself drew his sword upon these rebels. Every effort to induce them to stand having proved ineffectual, the force, exposed to a vastly superior fire of artillery, and completely out-flanked on both sides by an overpowering body of infantry and cavalry, which actually got into our rear, was compelled to retire with the loss of three pieces of artillery, which fell into the hands of the enemy, in consequence of the rank treachery of the Oude gunners, and with a very grievous list of killed and wounded. The heat was dreadful, the gun ammunition was expended, and the almost total want of cavalry to protect our rear made our retreat most disastrous.

"All the officers behaved well, and the exertions of the small body of Volunteer Cavalry — only forty in number—under Captain Radclyffe, 7th Light Cavalry, were most praiseworthy. Sir Henry Lawrence subsequently conveyed his thanks to myself, who had, at his request, accompanied him upon this occasion (Colonel Case being in command of Her Majesty's 32nd). He also expressed his approbation of the way in which his staff — Captain Wilson, Officiating Deputy Assistant Adjutant-General; Lieutenant James, Sub-Assistant Commissary-General; Captain Edgehill, Officiating Military Secretary; and Mr. Cooper,

Civil Service — the last of whom had acted as Sir Henry Lawrence's Aide-de-Camp from the commencement of the disturbances — had conducted themselves throughout this arduous day. Sir Henry further particularly mentioned that he would bring the gallant conduct of Captain Radclyffe and of Lieutenant Bonham, of the artillery (who worked the howitzer successfully until incapacitated by a wound), to the prominent notice of the Government of India. The manner in which Lieutenant Birch, 71st N. I., cleared a village with a party of Sikh skirmishers, also elicited the admiration of the Brigadier-General. The conduct of Lieutenant Hardinge, who, with his handful of horse, covered the retreat of the rear-guard, was extolled by Sir Henry, who expressed his intention of mentioning the services of this gallant officer to his Lordship in Council. Lieutenant-Colonel Case, who commanded Her Majesty's 32nd Regiment, was mortally wounded whilst gallantly leading his men. The service had not a more deserving officer. The command devolved on Captain Stevens, who also received a death-wound shortly afterwards. The command then fell to Captain Mansfield, who has since died of cholera. A list of the casualties on this occasion accompanies the despatch.

" It remains to report the siege operations.

" It will be in the recollection of his Lordship in Council that it was the original intention of Sir Henry Lawrence to occupy not only the Residency, but also the fort called the Muchee Bhawun, an old dilapidated edifice which had been hastily repaired for the occasion, though the defences were even at the last moment very far from complete, and were moreover commanded by many houses in the city.

The situation of the Muchee Bhawun with regard to the Residency has already been described to the Government of India.

" The untoward event of the 30th June so far diminished the whole available force, that we had not a sufficient number of men remaining to occupy both positions. The Brigadier-General, therefore, on the evening of the 1st July, signalled to the garrison of the Muchee Bhawun to evacuate and blow up that fortress in the course of the night. The orders were ably carried out, and at twelve P.M. the force marched into the Residency, with their guns and treasure, without the loss of a man ; and shortly afterwards the explosion of 240 barrels of gunpowder, and 6,000,000 ball-cartridges, which were lying in the magazine, announced to Sir Henry Lawrence and his officers, who were anxiously waiting the report, the complete destruction of that post and all that it contained. If it had not been for this wise and strategic measure, no member of the Lucknow garrison, in all probability, would have survived to tell the tale ; for, as has already been stated, the Muchee Bhawun was commanded from other parts of the town, and was moreover indifferently provided with heavy artillery ammunition, while the difficulty, suffering, and loss which the Residency garrison, even with the reinforcement thus obtained from the Muchee Bhawun, has undergone in holding the position, is sufficient to show that, if the original intention of holding both posts had been adhered to, both would inevitably have fallen.

" It is now my very painful duty to relate the calamity which befel us at the commencement of the siege. On the 1st July an 8-inch shell burst in the room in the Residency in which Sir H. Lawrence was sitting.

The missile burst between him and Mr. Cooper, close to both, but without injury to either. The whole of his staff implored Sir Henry to take up other quarters, as the Residency had then become the special target for the round shot and shell of the enemy. This, however, he jestingly declined to do, observing that another shell would certainly never be pitched into that small room. But Providence had ordained otherwise, for on the very next day he was mortally wounded by a fragment of another shell which burst in the same room, exactly on the same spot. Captain Wilson, Deputy-Assistant Adjutant-General, received a contusion at the same time.

"The late lamented Sir H. Lawrence, knowing that his last hour was rapidly approaching, directed me to assume command of the troops, and appointed Major Banks to succeed him in the office of chief commissioner. He lingered in great agony till the morning of the 4th July, when he expired, and the Government was thereby deprived, if I may venture to say so, of the services of a distinguished statesman and a most gallant soldier. Few men have ever possessed to the same extent the power which he enjoyed of winning the hearts of all those with whom he came in contact, and thus ensuring the warmest and most zealous devotion for himself and for the Government which he served. The successful defence of the position has been, under Providence, solely attributable to the foresight which he evinced in the timely commencement of the necessary operations, and the great skill and untiring personal activity which he exhibited in carrying them into effect. All ranks possessed such confidence in his judgment and his fertility of resource, that the news of his fall was received throughout the garrison with feelings of consternation, only second to the grief which was inspired in the hearts of all by the loss of a public benefactor and a warm personal friend. Feeling as keenly and as gratefully as I do the obligations that the whole of us are under to this great and good man, I trust the Government in India will pardon me for having attempted, however imperfectly, to portray them. In him every good and deserving soldier has lost a friend, and a chief capable of discriminating, and ever on the alert to reward merit, no matter how humble the sphere in which it was exhibited.

"The garrison had scarcely recovered the shock which it had sustained in the loss of its revered and beloved general, when it had to mourn the death of that able and respected officer, Major Banks, the officiating chief commissioner, who received a bullet through his head while examining a critical outpost on the 21st July, and died without a groan.

"The description of our position and the state of our defences when the siege began are so fully set forth in the accompanying memorandum, furnished by the garrison engineer, that I shall content myself with bringing to the notice of his Lordship in Council the fact that when the blockade was commenced only two of our batteries were completed, part of the defences were yet in an unfinished condition, and the buildings in the immediate vicinity, which gave cover to the enemy, were only very partially cleared away. Indeed, our heaviest losses have been caused by the fire from the enemy's sharpshooters stationed in the adjoining mosques and houses of the native nobility, the necessity of destroying which had been repeatedly drawn to the attention of Sir Henry

by the staff of engineers; but his invariable reply
was, 'Spare the holy places, and private property
too, as far as possible;' and we have consequently
suffered severely from our very tenderness to the
religious prejudices and respect to the rights of our
rebellious citizens and soldiery. As soon as the enemy
had thoroughly completed the investment of the Residency, they occupied these houses, some of which were
within easy pistol-shot of our barricades, in immense
force, and rapidly made loopholes on those sides which
bore on our post, from which they kept up a terrific
and incessant fire day and night, which caused many
daily casualties, as there could not have been less than
8,000 men firing at one time into our position. Moreover, there was no place in the whole of the works
that could be considered safe, for several of the sick
and wounded who were lying in the banqueting-hall,
which had been turned into a hospital, were killed in
the very centre of the building, and the widow of
Lieutenant Dorin and other women and children were
shot dead in a room into which it had not been previously deemed possible that a bullet could penetrate.
Neither were the enemy idle in erecting batteries.
They soon had from twenty to twenty-five guns in
position, some of them of very large calibre. These
were planted all round our post at small distances,
some being actually within fifty yards of our defences,
but in places where our own heavy guns could not
reply to them; while the perseverance and ingenuity
of the enemy in erecting barricades in front and around
their guns, in a very short time rendered all attempts
to silence them by musketry entirely unavailing.
Neither could they be effectually silenced by shells,
by reason of their extreme proximity to our position,

and because, moreover, the enemy had recourse to digging very narrow trenches about eight feet in depth in rear of each gun, in which the men lay while our shells were flying, and which so effectually concealed them, even while working the gun, that our baffled sharpshooters could only see their hands while in the act of loading.

" The enemy contented themselves with keeping up this incessant fire of cannon and musketry until the 29th of July, on which day, at ten A.M., they assembled in very great force all around our position, and exploded a heavy mine inside our outer line of defences at the Water-gate. The mine, however, which was close to the Redan, and apparently sprung with the intention of destroying that battery, did no harm; but as soon as the smoke had cleared away, the enemy boldly advanced under cover of a tremendous fire of cannon and musketry, with the object of storming the Redan. But they were received with such a heavy fire, that after a short struggle they fell back with much loss. A strong column advanced at the same time to attack Innes's post, and came on to within ten yards of the palisades, affording to Lieutenant Loughnan, 13th Native Infantry, who commanded the position, and his brave garrison, composed of gentlemen of the Uncovenanted Service, a few of Her Majesty's 32nd Foot and of the 13th Native Infantry, an opportunity of distinguishing themselves, which they were not slow to avail themselves of, and the enemy were driven back with great slaughter. The insurgents made minor attacks at almost every outpost, but were invariably defeated, and at two P.M. they ceased their attempts to storm the place, although their musketry fire and cannonading continued to harass us unceasingly as usual. Matters proceeded in this manner until the 10th of August, when the enemy made another assault, having previously sprung a mine close to the brigade mess, which entirely destroyed our defences for the space of twenty feet, and blew in a great portion of the outside wall of the house occupied by Mr. Schilling's garrison. On the dust clearing away, a breach appeared through which a regiment could have advanced in perfect order, and a few of the enemy came on with the utmost determination, but were met with such a withering flank fire of musketry from the officers and men holding the top of the brigade mess, that they beat a speedy retreat, leaving the more adventurous of their numbers lying on the crest of the breach. While this operation was going on, another large body advanced on the Cawnpore Battery, and succeeded in locating themselves for a few minutes in the ditch. They were, however, dislodged by hand grenades. At Captain Anderson's post they also came boldly forward with scaling ladders, which they planted against the wall; but here, as elsewhere, they were met with the most indomitable resolution, and, the leaders being slain, the rest fled, leaving the ladders, and retreated to their batteries and loopholed defences, from whence they kept up, for the rest of the day, an unusually heavy cannonade and musketry fire. On the 18th of August the enemy sprung another mine in front of the Sikh lines, with very fatal effect. Captain Orr (Unattached), Lieutenants Mecham and Soppitt, who commanded the small body of drummers composing the garrison, were blown into the air, but providentially returned to earth with no further injury than a severe shaking. The garrison, however, were not so fortunate. No less than eleven men were buried alive under the ruins, from whence it was impossible to extricate them, owing to the tremendous fire kept up by the enemy from houses situated not ten yards in front of the breach. The explosion was followed by a general assault of a less determined nature than the two former efforts, and the enemy were consequently repulsed without much difficulty. But they succeeded, under cover of the breach, in establishing themselves in one of the houses in our position, from which they were driven in the evening by the bayonets of Her Majesty's 32nd and 82nd Foot. On the 5th of September the enemy made their last serious assault. Having exploded a large mine, a few feet short of the bastion of the 18-pounder gun, in Major Apthorp's post, they advanced with large scaling ladders, which they planted against the wall, and mounted, thereby gaining for an instant the embrasure of a gun. They were, however, speedily driven back with loss, by hand grenades and musketry. A few minutes subsequently they sprung another mine close to the brigade mess, and advanced boldly; but soon the corpses strewed in the garden in front of the post bore testimony to the fatal accuracy of the rifle and musketry fire of the gallant members of that garrison, and the enemy fled ignominiously, leaving their leader—a fine-looking old native officer—among the slain. At other posts they made similar attacks, but with less resolution, and everywhere with the same want of success. Their loss upon this day must have been very heavy, as they came on with much determination, and at night they were seen bearing large numbers of their killed and wounded over the bridges in the direction of cantonments. The above is a faint attempt at a description of the four great struggles which have occurred during this protracted season of exertion, exposure, and suffering. His Lordship in Council will perceive that the enemy invariably commenced his attacks by the explosion of a mine—a species of offensive warfare for the exercise of which our position was unfortunately peculiarly situated, and had it not been for the most untiring vigilance on our part in watching and blowing up their mines before they were completed, the assaults would probably have been much more numerous, and might, perhaps, have ended in the capture of the place. But by countermining in all directions we succeeded in detecting and destroying no less than four of the enemy's subterraneous advances towards important positions, two of which operations were eminently successful, as on one occasion no less than eighty of them were blown into the air, and twenty suffered a similar fate on the second explosion. The labour, however, which devolved upon us in making these countermines, in the absence of a body of skilled miners, was very heavy. The Right Honourable the Governor-General in Council will feel that it would be impossible to crowd within the limits of a despatch even the principal events, much more the individual acts of gallantry which have marked this protracted struggle. But I can conscientiously declare my conviction, that few troops have ever undergone greater hardships, exposed as they have been to a never-ceasing musketry fire and cannonade. They have also experienced the alternate vicissitudes of extreme wet and of intense heat, and that too with very insufficient shelter from either, and in many places without any shelter at all. In addition to having to repel real attacks, they have been exposed night and day to the hardly less harassing false alarms which the enemy have been constantly raising. The insurgents have frequently fired very heavily, sounded the advance and shouted for several hours together, though not a man could be seen, with the view, of course, of harassing our small and exhausted force, in which object they succeeded, for no part has been strong enough to allow of a portion only of the garrison being prepared in the event of a false attack being turned into a real one. All, therefore, had to stand to their arms and to remain at their posts until the demonstration had ceased; and such attacks were of almost nightly occurrence. The whole of the officers and men have been on duty night and day during the eighty-seven days which the siege had lasted, up to the arrival of Sir J. Outram, G.C.B. In addition to this incessant military duty, the force has been employed in repairing defences, in moving guns, in burying dead animals, in conveying ammunition and commissariat stores from one place to another, and in other fatigue duties too numerous and too trivial to enumerate here. I feel, however, that any words of mine will fail to convey an adequate idea of what our fatigue and labours have been; labours in which all ranks and all classes—civilians, officers, and soldiers—have borne an equally noble part. All have together descended into the mine, all have together handled the shovel for the interment of the putrid bullock, and all, accoutred with musket and bayonet, have relieved each other on sentry, without regard to the distinction of rank civil or military. Notwithstanding all these hardships, the garrison has made no less than five sorties, in which they spiked two of the enemy's heaviest guns and blew up several of the houses from which they had kept up the most harassing fire. Owing to the extreme paucity of our numbers, each man was taught to feel that on his own individual efforts alone depended, in no small measure, the safety of the entire position. This consciousness incited every officer, soldier, and man to defend the post assigned to him with such desperate tenacity, and to defend the lives which Providence had entrusted to his care with such dauntless determination, that the enemy, despite their constant attacks, their heavy mines, their overwhelming numbers, and their incessant fire, could never succeed in gaining one single inch of ground within the bounds of this straggling position, which was so feebly fortified that had they once obtained a footing in any of the outposts the whole place must inevitably have fallen.

" If further proof be wanting of the desperate nature of the struggle which we have, under God's blessing, so long and so successfully waged, I would point to the roofless and ruined houses, to the crumbled walls, to the exploded mines, to the open breaches, to the shattered and disabled guns and defences, and lastly, to the long and melancholy list of the brave and devoted officers and men who have fallen. These silent witnesses bear sad and solemn testimony to the way in which this feeble position has been defended. During the early part of these vicissitudes, we were left without any information whatever regarding the posture of affairs outside. An occasional spy did indeed come in with the object of inducing our sepoys and servants to desert ; but the intelligence derived from such sources was of course entirely untrustworthy. We sent our messengers daily calling for aid and asking for information, none of whom ever returned until the twenty-sixth day of the siege, when a pensioner named Ungud, came back with a letter from General Havelock's camp, informing us that they were advancing with a force sufficient to bear down all opposition, and would be with us in five or six days. A messenger was immediately despatched, requesting that, on the evening of their arrival on the outskirts of the city, two rockets might be sent up, in order that we might take the necessary measures for assisting them while forcing their way in. The sixth day, however, expired, and they came not; but for many evenings after officers and men watched for the ascension of the expected rockets, with hopes such as make the heart sick. We knew not then, nor did we learn until the 29th of August — or thirty-five days later — that the relieving force, after having fought most nobly to effect our deliverance, had been obliged to fall back for reinforcements; and this was the last communication we received until two days before the arrival of Sir James Outram on the 25th of September.

"Besides heavy visitations of cholera and small-pox, we have also had to contend against a sickness which has almost universally pervaded the garrison. Commencing with a very painful eruption, it has merged into a low fever, combined with diarrhœa; and although few or no men have actually died from its effects, it leaves behind a weakness and lassitude which, in the absence of all material substances, save coarse beef and still coarser flour, none have been able entirely to get over. The mortality among the women and children, and especially among the latter, from these diseases, and from other causes, has been perhaps the most painful characteristic of the siege. The want of native servants has also been a source of much privation. Owing to the suddenness with which we were besieged, many of these people, who might, perhaps, have otherwise proved faithful to their employers, but who were outside the defences at the time, were altogether excluded. Very many more deserted, and several families were consequently left without the services of a single domestic. Several ladies have had to tend their children, and even to wash their own clothes, as well as to cook their scanty meals, entirely unaided. Combined with the absence of servants, the want of proper accommodation has probably been the cause of much of the disease with which we have been afflicted. I cannot refrain from bringing to the prominent notice of his Lordship in Council the patient endurance and the Christian resignation which have been evinced by the women of this garrison. They have animated us by their example. Many, alas! have been made widows, and their children fatherless, in this cruel struggle. But all such seem resigned to the will of Providence, and many, among whom may be mentioned the honoured names of Birch, of Polehampton, of Barber, and of Gall, have, after the example of Miss Nightingale, constituted themselves the tender and solicitous nurses of the wounded and dying soldiers in the hospital."

The Brigadier then enters into specific details of the services rendered by the most distinguished officers &c., whether living or dead. He also bears testimony to the unsurpassed courage and loyalty of the native troops; expresses the deep and grateful sense entertained by the garrison of the services rendered by Sir James Outram and General Havelock and their troops in effecting the relief of Lucknow at so heavy a sacrifice of life, and concludes with these words:—" We are also repaid for much suffering and privation by the sympathy which our brave deliverers say our perilous and unfortunate position has excited for us in the hearts of our countrymen throughout the length and breadth of Her Majesty's dominions."

THE END.

LONDON
PRINTED BY SPOTTISWOODE AND CO.
NEW-STREET SQUARE.

Printed in Great Britain by
Amazon.co.uk, Ltd.,
Marston Gate.